FATHERS
AND
SONS

FATHERS
AND
SONS

10 LIFE PRINCIPLES TO MAKE YOUR RELATIONSHIP STRONGER

RON & MATT JENSON

BROADMAN
& HOLMAN
PUBLISHERS

Nashville, Tennessee

© 1998 by Ron and Matt Jenson
All rights reserved
Printed in the United States of America
0-8054-1248-4
Published by Broadman & Holman Publishers, Nashville, Tennessee
Acquisitions & Development Editor: William D. Watkins
Dewey Decimal Classification: 306
Subject Heading: FATHERS AND SONS
Library of Congress Card Catalog Number: 97-50255

Unless otherwise stated all Scripture citation is from the New International Version, copyright © 1973, 1978, 1984 by the International Bible Society. Another version used is J. B. Phillips: *The New Testament in Modern English*, Revised Edition, © J. B. Phillips 1958, 1960, 1972; reprinted with permission of MacMillan Publishing Co., Inc.

Library of Congress Cataloging-in-Publication Data
Jenson, Ron, 1948–
    Fathers and sons : 10 life principles to make your relationship stronger /
by Ron and Matt Jenson.
       p. cm.
    Includes bibliographical references.
    ISBN 0-8054-1248-4 (pbk.)
    1. Fathers and sons. 2. Fathers and sons—Problems, exercises, etc. 3. Fathers and sons—Religious aspects—Christianity.
I. Jenson, Matt, 1976– . II. Title.
HQ755.85.J46   1998
306.874'2—dc21

                                        97-50255
                                           CIP

1 2 3 4 5 02 01 00 99 98

To our dad and grandad,
Bob Jenson,
for being a great example of a father
and for making his mark on our lives.

TABLE OF
CONTENTS

GETTING STARTED

It began ten years ago. We—Ron, the father, and Matt, the son—would meet at the local Bob's Big Boy restaurant and study the Book of Proverbs, looking for wisdom on how to live and how to relate to each other. Not that living wisely was easy, but relating to each other turned out to be particularly tricky.

When I (Ron) became a father, I began the struggle to be a good dad. I was intense about being a superdad, while Matt, my son, was just intense.

That gets us to me (Matt). I was a perfectionistic, driven, angry little kid. Add to those qualities my tendency to be introverted, and my parents knew they had their hands full.

So, what do you do with this combination?

The answer is *your best*. This book is all about fathers and sons growing together and doing their best at it. You see, child-rearing and dad-rearing are joint ventures. Fathers rear their sons, but as they do, sons also help their fathers mature. When the relationship works well, they support each other in their different roles, honoring each other and holding each other accountable. In the process, their relationship grows into a mutually satisfying friendship that can maximize the good times and weather the bad times in life.

We (Ron and Matt) know this is true. In our growing up together, we have experienced victories and defeats, but through it all, we have grown closer. Both of us have matured and strengthened as men, learning a great deal about each other and life along the way. Now that I (Matt) am in college, my dad and I feel encouraged by our father-son experience, saddened we didn't have more time together, hopeful for the future, and mournful over the prospect of my permanently leaving home after graduation to lead my own life. Even though it's a transition we eagerly anticipate for the excitement and sense of accomplishment that comes with it, it also carries with it a feeling of loss. It's yet another change we will have to grow through.

We want you to grow in your father-son relationship, too, which brings us to why we have written this book.

WHY THIS BOOK

The book you now hold has been ten years in the making. We started it in 1988, but found we had to work on it in spurts. We kept plugging away at it because of our desire to strengthen and deepen our father-son relationship and to help other fathers and sons do the same.

Throughout the course of writing this book, we encouraged each other, reminding ourselves of the goals we wanted to meet. First, we wanted to grow in our understanding, application, and integration of wisdom in our lives. I (Ron) have spent much of my life studying successful men and women around the world, reading hundreds of books, and identifying ten core principles that lead people to *Make a Life, Not Just a Living* (the name of the companion book to this work). These core principles have been the glue in our father-son relationship, which is why they serve as the foundation of the chapters in *Fathers and Sons*. I call these principles of life M.A.X.I.M.I.Z.E.R.S., and we present them here as guides and facilitators for fathers and sons to grow individually and together.

Second, we wrote this book to accomplish a significant, positive project together that would benefit fathers, sons, families, and communities. Aristotle believed that a good friendship was composed of two people with a common goal or vision in mind. We hope to impress on you the importance of fathers and sons moving toward the goal of maximizing their lives for the good of their family and community.

Third, we wanted to give fathers and sons a practical tool that would free them from the perfectionistic demands found in many self-help books. Dads and sons need the freedom to be real—not the expectation of being flawless—as they learn from each other. By providing a fun tool that stimulates important dialogue between fathers and sons (while allowing for appropriate disagreement), we want dads to realize that they can learn from their sons, and sons to understand that they need to have realistic expectations of their fathers. The father-son relationship is a two-way street with many curves, bumps, detours, and road hazards along the way. All will not go smoothly, but if fathers and sons give each other the freedom to be open and honest about their strengths, weaknesses, successes, and failures, the journey will bring long-lasting, life-changing rewards.

Our fourth reason for writing this book is that we wanted dads and sons to connect. George Bernard Shaw once said, "In the right key you can say anything, in the wrong key nothing. The only delicate part of life is the establishment of the key." Think about that for a moment. When the members of an orchestra are all playing in the right key, the music is beautiful. But when even one member of the orchestra tries playing in a different key, the music sounds horrible.

I (Ron) remember when my college orchestra got to perform a piece that would be conducted by its composer. As a trombonist, I was called on to play a unique part in the composition. During the orchestra's dress rehearsal, the conductor kept stopping at the same place in the music and shouting, "Someone is playing the wrong note!" He singled out the brass section as having the guilty party. Soon he narrowed the field to the trombones, then finally discovered that I was the musician making the rest of the orchestra sound bad. *Whoosh!* The conductor's wand sailed through the air, missing my head by just inches. He knew how important it was that I played the right note, and he was going to make certain that I understood it too.

Similarly, playing in the same key in the father-son relationship is extremely important. When you both play in harmony, you are connecting and communicating. No overt offense occurs between the two of you because you are caring for each other and keeping short accounts by dealing quickly and appropriately with any hurts that spring up between you.

If you don't work at staying in this spirit of unity, you might as well forget trying to grow together. Being united is the heart of the issue. By taking a few minutes to work through some of these issues in this book, you can keep reconnecting and stay in the right key, making your journey together more than worthwhile.

MAXIMIZING THIS BOOK

This book is a personal growth tool more than anything else. We want you to grow together using whatever suggestions you find helpful. Try the I.D.E.A. method of education. IDEA is an acronym (a word formed by combining the initial letters of a series of words) for the following:

Instruction. Education happens best in a life-related situation. Therefore, we urge you to read one chapter at a time and interact on the content. Talk about how it relates to your life context. We will recommend additional readings and tapes for further help should you desire it.

Demonstration. Many of us learn best by watching models or examples of healthy behavior. In this book, we have provided our father-son relationship as a model, and we ask that you learn from our positive and negative experiences. We don't present ourselves as two men who have it all together. We are in process as you are. Our lives are still under construction. However, we believe we have traveled the road far enough to use our own experience to help guide and prepare you for the journey.

Experience. *Doing* is where education becomes real. It's one thing
to parrot back information but quite another to practice it. We
will urge you to do exercises to build qualities into your lives that
will help you grow together. Remember, Dad, you are not just
the teacher; you are the learner as well. So learn from the materials and your son. And Son, relax and grow with your dad.

Assessment. Someone has said, "People don't do what you expect
but what you inspect." The real power in this book is in the
times you meet to evaluate the material. We recommend that
you commit to go through this book working on one chapter
every one or two weeks. Go out for a breakfast or lunch meeting
and share your insights, read your answers to the action steps,
and grow together. Covering the content is important, but the
main goal is to build a relationship as father and son. This means
listening and understanding each other, which requires asking
questions and trying to see how the other person feels. Remember, your dad or son is not your enemy; you are on the same
team. So work together, be patient, and don't worry about the
initial awkwardness. Just do it!

As you'll see, each chapter contains several sessions designed to
help you develop different aspects of the ten MAXIMIZERS principles. At the end of each session, you will find a section called "Putting This to Work" where we provide very practical steps for
interacting with the material and applying it to your lives individually and together. We use the following symbols to communicate
what should be done:

✎   *Write*—Use this workbook to answer individually.

📖   *Read*—Do this individually or together.

☞   *Talk*—Set a time to get together just to talk. Don't talk while
you clean the garage, sort your laundry, do your taxes, and so

forth. Pay attention—giving and getting something out of your time together.

✓ Act—Decide together on a plan of action, then practice individually and encourage each other to make the principles you're learning a part of your life.

At the end of each chapter will be a section called "Final Project," which focuses on one major aspect of the principle under discussion. You'll find that directions and space are provided for you to follow each Final Project for twenty-one days straight. The reason for this time commitment is that habits take time to develop. Many social scientists assert that twenty-one days of consistent practice results in the initial establishment of a habit. It's when the MAXIMIZERS principles become habitual in your lives that lasting, positive change will occur. We give you a simple log to record the results of your work in making the MAXIMIZERS principles lifetime habits.

MORE TIPS FOR THE ROAD

As you work through *Fathers and Sons*, remember that the goal is meaningful communication and growth, so don't get bogged down trying to follow a rigorous schedule. Pick whatever method meshes with your continuing study. You could jump from session to session, choosing the sessions that best suit where the two of you are right now. For example, if you want to build some discipline in your life, do session 2, "Be Disciplined, Not Lazy," in chapter 2. Or you could do one session when you get together each week. Then after you're done with the sessions of a given chapter, spend the next twenty-one days on the Final Project—either continuing with the sessions of the next chapter while doing the Final Project, or waiting to finish the twenty-one-day project, and then moving on to the next chapter.

Your goal is not to blaze through the book in record time, but to grow together as father and son. So if you find you need to spend a lot of extra time working through a chapter, do it. We wrote each session so it could be done in thirty to forty-five minutes, but if you need more time, take it. You set the pace and let this book be your servant, not your master.

You might consider using this book as a growth tool over a two- to four-year period. After all, what's the rush? Feel free to take your time. A two- to four-year plan will allow you to work at a comfortable pace of a session every two to four weeks. Frankly, if you want to see real change take place, it will take that kind of time to build the life skill we develop in each chapter.

We also encourage you to get Ron's book, *Make a Life, Not Just a Living* (Broadman & Holman Publishers, 1997), which, as previously mentioned, expands on each of the ten core principles that underlie *Fathers and Sons*. Ron has also developed a video and audio series on these principles, providing even more background and understanding. (These materials can be ordered from Future Achievement International using the address provided in the back of this book.)

We urge you to adapt this book to meet your needs. For instance, although we wrote this book for dads to use with their sons who are in junior high or high school, the material could be adapted to younger and older ages as well. Moreover, some dads who have used earlier versions of the material in this book have involved all their children (both boys and girls) and found it quite helpful. Couples, single parents, and grandfathers could also adapt this work. If you are or would like to become an adopted dad for a fatherless child, you could also use this book to develop that relationship. We could likewise see fathers and sons adapting this material for use in father-son groups. Even older adult sons and fathers have told us about their intentions of using *Fathers and Sons* to build or perhaps rebuild bridges between them. In short, this book's primary purpose is to serve your needs in your situation. So shape it and apply it as you need.

Finally, although we wrote this book so people of any or no religious persuasion could profit from it, we want you to know that we are Christians and that we find a great deal of guidance for our lives in the Bible, which we believe is God's written word to humanity. We have occasionally provided exercises in *Fathers and Sons* that include reading, meditating on, discussing, and applying biblical passages. But we realize that you may not share our religious perspective, and if that's the case, feel free to skip these exercises. Before you do, though, we would ask you to consider the possibility that you can still find insight in the Bible's pages that could help maximize your life and your father-son relationship, whether you believe the Bible is God's Word or not.

For centuries, people of various religious and philosophical persuasions have found the Bible to be a rich source of time-tested wisdom, benefiting from it even though they believe it is but a human book. Virtually all of America's founders saw the value of applying biblical principles to life. For instance, James Madison, the architect of the U.S. Constitution, said, "We have staked the whole future of American civilization, not upon the power of government, far from it. We have staked the future of all of our political institutions upon the capacity of mankind for self-government; upon the capacity of each and all of us to govern ourselves, to control ourselves, to sustain ourselves *according to the Ten Commandments of God*" (italics added).

Just as you can derive benefit from reading works by the great thinkers and leaders of today, so can you by reading the great works of the past. The Bible is one of the best sources of ancient, timeless wisdom. It contains the works of some of the finest leaders (e.g., Moses, David, and Nehemiah), poets (Job and Deborah), military strategists (Joshua), historians (Luke), social analysts (Hosea and Amos), philosophers (Solomon), and theologians (Paul and John) who ever lived. This is certainly one reason for its incredible popularity and influence. After all, the Bible is the number one best-seller of all time.

Since so many people over so many centuries have found help for their lives in the Bible, perhaps you could too. We know that we certainly have.

Enough said. It's now your turn to start growing together. Enjoy the journey!

Feel free to write or fax us a note to let us know how this book is working for you. We would like to share your experience with our family and friends around the world. You can use the address and fax information at the end of this book. Thanks.

CHAPTER ONE

WHAT'S A DAD AND SON TO DO?

A dad approaches his son and asks, "Why don't you do what I say?"

"Whatever," says the son. "Why don't you ever spend time with me?"

"I'm busy and you know it," the dad responds.

"Yeah, you're busy . . . too busy for your own son."

That painful exchange happens too much today. And whether you two have had words like that or not, this dialogue reflects the kind of expectations we all have for one another.

Dads want their sons to respect and obey them. Sons want time, encouragement, and respect from their dads.

What are your expectations for yourself and your son or dad? By the way, you will find us urging you to focus on your own responsibilities, not those of your dad or son. Hey, you can't control how your dad or son responds to his responsibilities, but you can take responsibility to be the best dad or son you can be. If you will focus on these root responsibilities, you are much more likely to get the fruit in your relationship that you really need and desire.

Let's begin by examining how we each see our own role and what we expect of the other person.

THE DAD'S ROLE: THE SON'S PERSPECTIVE

Above all, I (Matt) think the father must be the model for what he wishes his son to be, showing what a good father, husband, and person is like. So be aware: when the son sees his father in action, he will be deciding if he wants to grow up to be like Dad or unlike Dad.

Also, boys retain and react more to something their fathers do rather than something their fathers say to do. For example, if a son sees his dad lying to a business associate, the son will completely discard the speech on integrity his father gave him a week ago. Hypocrisy doesn't wash with kids.

Fathers should be strong and confident, but they should also be willing to show an occasional chink in the armor. Sons don't expect perfection, although they do expect a sincere attempt at it.

In addition, the father needs to tangibly express his love for his son. Sons need to be hugged often.

The father also needs to verbally express his love for his son. All the fathers I know love their sons, but I can think of only a handful who know how to express emotion-laden commitment. A bit of inside advice: Forget the ego, and simply say, "I love you, son." Say those four words specifically, not something like, "Son, you know how much you mean to me, right?" Men and boys don't believe something unless they hear it point-blank and word-for-word. Sons need to hear "I love you" often.

Sons also need to be respected. A father should not say, "I'm your father. You have to respect me," and not give that respect in return. Fathers need to earn that respect.

Most of all, a father should be willing to learn from his son!

THE DAD'S PERSPECTIVE

When I (Ron) think about the roles of dads and sons, I think of basic attitudes. I use the D.A.D. acronym to communicate what I think a dad should be.

Devoted. Dads need to be devoted to the most important things in life. For me this includes my relationship with God, my marriage, my family, and my overall values and ethics. The *American Heritage Dictionary* defines "devoted" as "to give or apply (one's time, attention, or self) entirely to a particular activity, pursuit, cause, or person. To set apart . . . a vow or solemn act; dedicate; consecrate."

As dads we need to give our time and attention to priorities that reflect the lifestyle we want to model to our sons. We need to be devoted—dedicated and consecrated—to our sons. But we also need to be devoted to our God and our wife and the other priorities we want our sons to adopt.

Affirming. Encouragement, belief, expectation, support—all of these words help to explain affirmation. Sons need to be affirmed. Some time ago a national family council surveyed parents about how many positive versus negative statements they made to their children. The council discovered that the average parent said ten negative statements for every positive statement.

Such a ratio is one of the reasons why we are in so much trouble as a culture. People grow, mature, and reach their potential as they are affirmed. People build much of their sense of self-worth based on affirmation or lack of it. Sons get enough harrassment and negative input from their peers and the culture at large. Fathers need to counteract that negative input, not add to it.

Some years ago, a substitute teacher came into one of the toughest classrooms in the inner city of New York. He radically turned around a class of troublemakers with failing grades. At the end of the year, he received an award for his incredible work. The principal asked him how he could get so much out of such unmotivated, uneducated kids. The teacher responded, "I don't know what you mean. These kids are bright. Here, just look at their IQs." The principal glanced at the numbers that came from the previous teacher's class book, then said, "Those aren't their IQs. Those are their locker numbers."

But because the teacher thought the kids were bright and treated them as such, they responded to his expectations and encouragement.

As dads we need to elevate our sons' belief in themselves by articulating praise, not tearing them down; and expressing confidence, not demeaning their attempts. We also need to demonstrate affection. Remember, the nonverbal part of communications is more than 80 percent of the game. There is power in a hug and a kiss. Matt is now twenty-one and we still do both.

Deliberate. Dads tend to be passive at best and abusive at worst in their relationships with their sons, often replaying whatever role their own fathers modeled for them. That model may have been terrific or terrible. If we don't reenact our father's model (as many of us do despite our intentions to never be like our fathers), we overreact to it and go to the other extreme. For instance, it is not uncommon for a man who was reared in an extremely permissive environment to become a strict disciplinarian to his own son.

If we dads are deliberate, we will take the initiative to love, care for, coach, build up, shepherd, pray for, enjoy, and mentor our sons. We won't wait for a crisis but will develop goals, basic values, and strategies to be the kinds of dads we ought to be. Otherwise, our sons will leave home with deep disappointment and pain—and we will both wish we could do it over again.

THE SON'S ROLE: THE SON'S PERSPECTIVE

Both the father and the son should drop their egos immediately. If either wants a strong relationship with the other, he must have an open mind. Egos will just stop the whole process. Most important, sons, you need to realize that your father loves you. As strange as it may seem, your father is doing his utmost to raise you in the way he thinks will be best for you.

I (Matt) don't think the problem with father-son relationships has to do with a lack of love from either the son or the father. However, I think very few fathers and sons know how to express this love. You have to be honest with your dad. Make him someone you confide in. Very few things could encourage your father and help your relationship with him more than your sharing your thoughts, dreams, and fears with him.

Take some time to get to know your father. If he is doing this study with you, it's likely he is as interested as you—if not more so—in sharing and growing together.

I often think of my dad as some kind of superman who can't be hurt by anything or anyone. But that's far from the truth. My dad is a great guy, but he also has weaknesses and fears. He's not perfect.

Your dad isn't perfect either. He messes up and is probably scared about how he is doing as a father. But he is trying as hard as he can and he loves you—so give him some respect based on those facts. In respecting him, you don't have to agree on everything, but realize that he has had more experience than you. Give his perspective a chance. In fact, it's vital that you look at things through your father's eyes and attempt to understand his emotions and motives. Your overall outlook on the relationship can improve. As a matter of fact, any time you take the focus off your own rights and place it on your responsibility to others, your attitude will improve . . . and so will your impact.

THE DAD'S PERSPECTIVE

Sons who want to improve their father-son relationships have three qualities.

Openness. We fathers greatly appreciate our sons' willingness to share their lives with us. The sharing brings us closer together as we learn what is going on in our sons' lives, and we get a better idea of how we can relate to each other. Many times we dads stay away from active fathering because we simply don't know what to do. We focus on work because that is where we are rewarded and affirmed—and because we know what we're doing there. In fact, many dads get their sense of worth only through work. That isn't healthy, but it is too often reality.

You can help your dad by being open with him. Learn to share your good news and bad news. Share your struggles and ask about his. Mostly, keep giving him a chance. Remember, this territory is tough for him.

Obedience. Sons need to obey dads! Ask your dad for his wisdom, insight, and guidance. Then listen to it and obey it. As you get older and your dad gets wiser, you will earn more freedom to choose your own direction. Obey him because you love your dad and want to affirm and respect him.

By the way, there is a lot of ugliness in our world today. Certainly, if you have a physically abusive dad (I don't mean just spanking), your mother or other friends need to protect you and you need to speak up. But unless there is an obvious abuse of honorable behavior on the part of your dad, obey—even if it seems unfair.

Neediness. Let your dad know you need him. Often, we dads are intimidated by our wives in the area of parenting. Moms and children bond early, relating so much better than we do. We have never had a course on parenting and so we often feel inadequate. And we dads like to work where we excel and feel needed.

Let your dad know you need him. Ask him questions, seek him out, jump in his lap (unless you are twice his size). Tell him you love him and realize that this will probably be easier for you to say than for him. But don't stop!

Putting This to Work

✎   1. What do you know about your dad/son? What kind of
        childhood would he say he had and why? What kinds of
        things does he like to do? What exactly does your dad do
        for a living? What exactly is your son involved in at school
        or in his free time?

        _____

        _____

        _____

        _____

        _____

        _____

        _____

        _____

        _____

        _____

        _____

☞   2. What is your definition of a dad? Of a son? Be as honest and
        direct as possible.

☞   3. Come together over a breakfast or another time away from
        the home. Read out loud what the other one wrote. Avoid
        defensive words or long explanations. Answer these ques-
        tions:

- How well do I know my dad/son?
- What points can we agree on concerning the role of dad and son?
- How am I doing in accomplishing my role?
- How can I improve this?
- Where do we both need improvement?
- How can I help you accomplish your proper role?

Make a commitment to support one another through encouraging words and actions!

CHAPTER TWO

MAKE THINGS HAPPEN

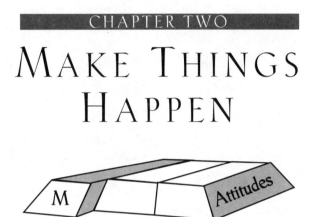

The first MAXIMIZERS principle for improving the relationship between fathers and sons is to make things happen. It is a responsibility principle that concerns attitude and has two aspects that we will examine:

- Be proactive, not reactive

- Be disciplined, not lazy

SESSION 1:
BE PROACTIVE, NOT REACTIVE

Do you remember the last time someone "pushed your buttons" by saying or doing something that made you irritated and defensive?

Ron remembers becoming sarcastic with Matt after an offensive comment on the basketball court. The ball was knocked out-of-bounds, and Ron called it out on the other team. Matt, who was on the other team, jumped in and said, "No way. It was out on you!"

"I didn't touch it," stated Ron.

"Yes, you did," responded Matt.

"Fine, you take it," said Ron in a less than kind voice.

Then, right as Matt was taking what could have been the winning shot, Ron said, out of frustration and in front of Matt's friends, "So you're calling me a liar."

Matt *did* make the shot, and his team won the game. Unfortunately, buttons were pushed on both sides.

Why did this happen? Ron often reacts to Matt's perfectionism and occasional black-and-white statements. In the heat of competition his reaction was even worse. So when Matt insisted the ball was out on Ron—whether Ron knew he touched it or not—Ron's buttons were pushed and he reacted.

The good news is that we have both learned enough to apologize for our inappropriate and hurtful actions and words, and we did just that shortly after this event.

The problem with most of us is that we let our buttons get pushed. We blame the other person and don't take responsibility for our own lives. This session deals with taking responsibility for ourselves by being proactive, not just reacting to others and life.

If you want to be successful, you have to decide right now to take charge of your life. Being proactive means doing something! This doesn't mean that if you go outside and weed out your backyard you're being proactive. Being proactive means doing something that accomplishes something meaningful. It's not just keeping busy.

Anyone can be busy, but how many people do you know who are proactive and accomplishing things?

People who accomplish significant objectives have a goal in mind. To make things happen and be proactive, you must also have a goal. Remember that the goals you set are meant to improve you, not your father/son. Be responsible for your own behavior improvement. For instance, sons, you may think your dads need to stop blaming you for things, but you have to realize that the only thing you can control is yourself. Dads, you may feel like your sons aren't responding to your guidance. Remember that you can only give the best guidance you can, and you can control your response to him; but you can't make your son listen and obey. He may appear to accept your guidance when he's with you, but rejects it and does his own thing when he's out of your sight and reach.

Don't waste your time trying to "fix" your dad or your son. This isn't to say that you can't tell your dad what you feel like when he blames you or tell your son what you feel like when he disobeys you. But the only thing you can really do is focus on you, becoming the most loving and responsible son/dad you can be. Worrying about problems you can't solve is like leaving the car battery running without driving anywhere. The battery's going to run down, and so are you. If you focus on what you *can* change, however, it's like turning on the car and driving somewhere. You are making things happen, and, like the car battery, you are continually recharging yourself.

When you focus on what you can change, you focus on the roots, not just the fruit. Focusing on the roots (right attitude, belief, commitment) of your life will help you make things happen. After all, if you focus just on the fruit (happiness, success, circumstances), you'll get impatient and frustrated waiting to see it happen. You'll try to force the fruit to show up, and it won't. If you focus on the roots, then the fruit will come in season.

Putting This to Work

1. What is a button in your life that is pushed by the other person? When was the last time it was pushed? How did you react? What areas of responsibility did *you* have? In other words, what could *you* control? What could you not control?

_____

_____

_____

_____

_____

_____

_____

_____

2. How can you be a more proactive (taking initiative to solve a problem) dad/son? Brainstorm this together. Come up with a list of at least five ways to improve. Write them down and then circle the one you both agree needs the most work. Now, remember this point: your job is to help one another grow, so don't be defensive if the other person brings up an area you think is OK. Instead, ask, "How do you see me act

like this? Can you give me a specific example?" The goal is
to authentically succeed by helping one another grow.

1. _____

2. _____

3. _____

4. _____

5. _____

3. Read Genesis 39 together. How did Joseph react in prison?

4. Write down one new practice (thought, attitude, word, or
   deed) you will commit to work on this week. Share this
   area and specific action with each other and agree to
   encourage one another in developing this into a habit.

_____

_____

_____

_____

_____

_____

_____

SESSION 2: BE DISCIPLINED, NOT LAZY

Ron was walking through the local Sears store with a friend some
years ago when—out of the blue—his friend turned to him and spat

in his face. That's right. Ron didn't say anything but kept walking, when again his friend spat in his face. This *is* a true story. Honest. Again, Ron kept silent after wiping his face and just waited for some type of comment but nothing was said. A few minutes later, Ron's friend looked at him with a stupid grin and spat in his face a third time. Then do you know what Ron did?

Nothing! Do you know why? His friend was his then six-month-old baby boy Matt.

"Now," you say, "that's a dumb story." Well, it has a point. When you thought we were talking about an adult, you were disgusted and shocked at his behavior. But when we said it was a baby, you thought nothing of it. Why?

Babies aren't trained to behave maturely. But adults are disciplined to act like mature people—not face spitters.

This session is all about your own discipline.

The second key to making things happen is to be disciplined, not lazy. Discipline is being able to control your life by having a sense of priorities, by putting first things first. Discipline governs thoughts and actions. In discipline, we have to work hard and develop right habits.

Basically, the entire concept of discipline is painful. To most people, it means not doing what they want to do, and consequently not having fun. That's false. Discipline is rewarding and fulfilling. As Albert Camus said, "Without work, all life becomes rotten." The hard work part of discipline is what people don't like. In reality, though, we always work hard—even if we're just working hard at relaxing!

People eagerly work for something they really want. If you want to maximize your life and improve your father-son relationship, then you will have to work at it. Don't work just to be busy. Your work should help you become a better son or a better father.

Along with the hard work must come the development of right habits. There is no point in working hard at bad habits. Habits must be good ones. Aristotle remarked, "We are what we repeatedly do." In other words, our little choices become habits over time and then we become those habits. Spooky huh? Now, that can be good news or bad news depending on the kind of habit we cultivate.

If you practice good habits today, then you will have a successful day. Now, we don't mean to say that everything will go your way or you'll get everything you want. Life isn't that simple. But you will be more productive and effective and will see desireable results in many vital areas of life.

If you practice bad habits, then you will have a lesser likelihood of real success and productivity, and, over time, your daily behavior will effect your weekly behavior and so on until the end of your life, as depicted in the chart below.

You can't just get rid of a bad habit; you need to replace it with the opposite, positive habit. If you struggle with your temper, for instance, you need to replace that lack of controlled temper with the habit of patience.

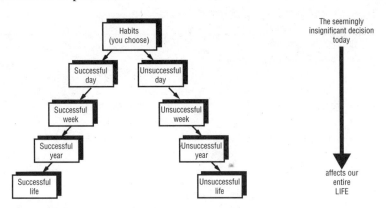

So, how do you build a habit? You starve your old bad habit and replace it with the new habit, making sure to feed the new habit daily. Let's say you have a problem with an inappropriate response to your anger—you blow up and say things you shouldn't. First decide to stop doing this, then replace the old reaction with kindness, gentleness, and thoughtfulness. Practice this new behavior in your mind over and over again. Envision yourself behaving as you want to, just as athletes envision themselves winning a competition (e.g., runners see themselves firmly planting their feet with each long stride, straining and pounding the course with all their might, eventually crossing the finish line in first place). You may even want to role-play this with your dad or son. Then, when you are tempted to react inappropriately, you apply the right behavior. The key is to do this for at least twenty-one days consistently and persistently. Once you have practiced this new behavior for this extended period of time, you will find the new habit becoming your response.

Putting This to Work

✎   1. What is your most irritating habit?

_____

_____

_____

_____

_____

_____

_____

2. What is your father's/son's most irritating habit?

_____

_____

_____

_____

_____

_____

_____

_____

3. Share your answers with your father/son. Remember to discuss this as friends, keeping words positive and constructive, not condemning.

4. In what specific ways can your father/son help motivate you to build this habit?

_____

_____

_____

_____

_____

_____

_____

To develop good habits, practice the following three steps:

- Step 1: Write down the positive habit you want to develop.

- Step 2: Four times a day (breakfast, lunch, dinner, and bedtime), mentally rehearse the habit. Think about it, dwell upon it, and practice it over and over in your mind.

- Step 3: Do your best to stay away from circumstances or situations that encourage the bad habit or discourage the positive habit.

5. What information or knowledge do you need to overcome this bad habit? For instance, if your temper is your bad habit, find books or articles on how to control your temper.

6. Read Proverbs 5:12, 14, 22–23. What is the result of a life without discipline?

FINAL PROJECT: MAKE THINGS HAPPEN

Identify one new habit you want to develop. Report to each other daily on how you observe your habit being formed. Keep a log. For instance, if you want to stop complaining, note your progress each day; e.g., "Day 1: I caught myself complaining twice today, but stopped once I realized what I was doing. Day 2: I asked Dad to remind me when he saw me complaining by scratching his nose."

Day	Progress
1	_____
2	_____
3	_____
4	_____
5	_____
6	_____
7	_____
8	_____
9	_____
10	_____
11	_____
12	_____
13	_____
14	_____
15	_____
16	_____
17	_____
18	_____
19	_____
20	_____
21	_____

CHAPTER THREE

ACHIEVE
PERSONAL
SIGNIFICANCE

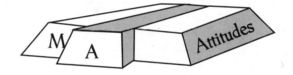

SESSION 1:
WHAT YOU SEE
IS WHAT YOU'LL BE

Once there was a boy who was extremely thin and painfully shy. He wanted to be tough and bulky, but no matter how many milk shakes and banana splits he downed, he couldn't gain a pound. To make matters worse, he was a minister's son—an inhibiting factor for somebody growing up in a small Ohio town. Practically every member of his family was a performer in public, which was the last thing he wanted to be.

"I was shy and bashful," he says, "and this self-image of inadequacy might have gone on indefinitely had it not been for something a professor said to me during my sophomore year in college. One day after I had made a miserable showing, he told me to wait after class. 'How long are you going to be bashful like this, a scared rabbit afraid of the sound of your own voice?' he demanded. 'You'd better change the way you think about yourself, Peale, before it's too late.'"

That may sound like a strong dose of medicine for the young boy, but it worked. The boy's name was Norman Vincent Peale, and he went on to become one of America's most popular preachers and writers.

You'd better change the way you think about yourself. Is it really possible to make such a change? After that encounter, Peale says, something *did* change: "The inferiority feelings were not all gone; I have some of them to this day. But I changed the *image* I had of myself—and with it the course of my life."[1]

There is no doubt that how we view ourselves largely determines how we live. If, for instance, you like who you are and what you see in the mirror, you will live a life that is positive and productive. If you don't, you won't. Our self-concept is crucial, and it needs to be based on our personal character and relevant to our mission and goals in life.

Matt was at the top of his class in sixth grade. Still, he came home from school half the time literally weeping about the day. Even though he was intelligent, he dreaded the thought of going to school each day and being teased with, "There's Matt Williams!" by the resident bullies. (Matt Williams, then the third baseman for the San Francisco Giants, only batted .188 that year. Ironically, he later became one of the Giant's great power hitters. But that happened many years after Matt Jenson was in the sixth grade.) Matt was academically confident, but he was socially miserable. He wanted nothing more than to be popular like those guys. He thought that because he was teased by everyone, he deserved the mockery. After all, if someone hears anything over and over, he will end up believing it. It's natural for people to take what's repeatedly said about them as the absolute truth, even if what's said is false and destructive.

Because Matt was frequently made fun of, he ended up thinking of himself as a dorky little nerd. Matt took everything these people said straight to heart. In retrospect, he realizes that none of these people knew who he was on the inside and that they were merely responding from their own insecurities. What's more, they probably didn't even realize the pain they were causing.

When Matt was playing piano in church recently, he saw one of the bullies that tormented him in sixth grade. Matt remembered his name and recalled a lot of things the guy had said to him. When Matt went up to him, eager to show that he was now confident, the bully hardly remembered him.

In a lot of ways, our society has become so pessimistic that it communicates the message that the individual is basically meaningless. But we have to live in light of who we truly are, not who people say we are. We have to get over this negative self-concept and realize that we can make a difference in the world. You *can* make a difference, and you start by achieving a true humility—one that recognizes both strengths and weaknesses and seeks to work with them accordingly.

Also, knowing that both negative and positive words impact people, focus on building up your father or son instead of tearing him down with negative comments. Be constructive, not destructive.

How do you suppose our self-concept is formed? Words, experiences, family, background, school, and friends can positively and negatively affect our view of ourselves.

The one thing Matt has had to learn is that not everyone is going to like him. Matt is, in general, a well-liked individual, but an insult by one person can tend to throw his whole self-concept out of whack.

Such an incident occurred one time during a school-wide assembly, while he was playing the part of Tommy Titan the Terminator in front of about fifteen hundred teenagers. The music was cued a little late, so Matt was left standing on stage in an awkward silence. All of a sudden, from the top of the bleachers, some guy yelled out, "Freak!" Needless to say, this was an embarrassing moment. What's more, a lot of people started laughing. Matt looked over at the spot where the insult had flown from, filled with rage, but he resisted the desire to lose his temper. At first, Matt felt pretty low. *Here is a bunch of people who clearly don't like me and think I'm a loser*, he thought. But then, when he thought about it a little more, he realized that this was just an isolated incident. Just because one person disliked him wasn't enough of a reason to think himself a failure.

In the same way, we cannot rely on individual opinions to dictate our own self-concept. When we get our sense of self-worth from others, it ceases to be self-worth at all, and is, instead, solely a subjective attitude based on the particular biases of other people. To combat this subjective attitude, fathers and sons can build each other's self-concept by focusing on one another's strengths.

Putting This to Work

1. How do you see yourself?

   - One word to characterize what I was like as a child is
     _____.

   - One word to characterize what I was like as a teenager is
     _____.

   - One word to characterize what I was like as a new
     employee is _____.

   - One word to characterize what I am like now is
     _____.

   - One word to characterize what I will be in the future is
     _____.

2. Consider how your self-concept has been built. What is
   one experience (like the incident from Matt's sixth grade
   year) that affected how you see yourself?

   _____

   _____

   _____

   _____

   _____

   _____

   _____

   _____

3. List three things you appreciate about your dad/son.

   1. _____

     _____

   2. _____

     _____

   3. _____

     _____

4. In your time together, share the words, experiences, and qualities you have written above. Take turns going first on each topic. Remember to be honest and nonjudgmental.

5. Read Psalm 139:1–6, 13–16. What does this text say about who you are?

SESSION 2:
YOU ARE SIGNIFICANT

In the words of Oliver Wendell Holmes: "The biggest tragedy in America is not the great waste of natural resources, though this is tragic. The greatest tragedy is the waste of human resources. The average person goes to his grave with his music still in him."

Is this the case with you? Are your resources in relationships, skills, and your life still untapped? What's keeping you from making your mark on the world? It's easy for us to say, "You need to have significance in your life!" But such a statement proves incredibly daunting. After all, what is significance, and how do I find it? Basically, significance refers to the meaningfulness of someone's life. This meaningfulness can occur in all sorts of ways, but it is always manifested when you have an impact on the world around you. Significance is others-centered, not me-centered.

To achieve real significance in your life and in the lives of others, you need to see that you really are special. You may picture Dana Carvey's church lady on *Saturday Night Live* saying, "Well, isn't that special?" Well, you are special. You are the only you there will ever be. And you were uniquely created to make a unique contribution. A gospel singer has said, "God don't make no junk." You're not junk. You are a treasure!

Dad, you have the remarkably special position to be your son's hero and mentor. Son, you are so special that your dad has dedicated his life to see you succeed in your own life. Each of you has unique abilities and a special way of expressing yourself that can achieve a significant impact on the world. Your job is not to be like each other. Your job is to be the best you can be. You are both unique. Develop and appreciate your own uniqueness and that of the other.

Putting This to Work

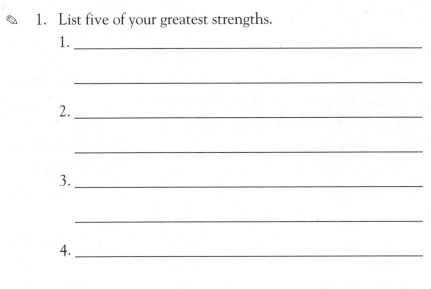

1. List five of your greatest strengths.

   1. _____

      _____

   2. _____

      _____

   3. _____

      _____

   4. _____

      _____

5. _____

_____

☞ 2. In your time together, share what you believe are your strengths. Then let your dad/son tell you if he sees other strengths as well. Talk about how you see each other's strengths and where they are practiced.

☞ 3. Consider together how you can be a support in cultivating these strengths. How can you encourage each other, help each other grow in these strengths, and learn from each other?

📖 4. Read Philippians 4:13. What is your power source? Does it work?

SESSION 3:
YOU CAN MAKE A DIFFERENCE

At the end of World War II, a celebration was held in the Los Angeles Colosseum. More than one hundred thousand people attended the program to honor the city's war heroes. Suddenly the lights went out, bringing the festivities to a grinding halt. Then a voice spoke out in the darkness: "You may think you are unimportant, that your job has no significance, but watch." The speaker struck a match. The tiny flame could be seen by everyone. "Now I'd like each one of you to do the same," he said. The audience gasped as one hundred thousand pinpoints of light illuminated the entire colosseum. That shows the impact of the effort of individuals.

With a fragile ego and low self-esteem, it's easy for us to think that we could never amount to anything. *Wrong!* We are convinced that anyone can have an impact. You can't stay home and sit on your duff, though. You have to get involved. That's the key. You have to care enough to try to make a difference. So what kind of difference are you making?

Putting This to Work

1. For this exercise you will need seven 3" x 5" cards. On each of the seven cards, list a past achievement you feel was positive. List experiences in which you felt a sense of real satisfaction or enjoyment. Include big things and little things—anything that felt satisfying or brought you closer to achieving a goal (e.g., projects, speeches, reports, chairing a meeting, solving a problem). Don't look for dramatic or unusual examples.

   On the back of each of your seven cards, write a paragraph describing the experience. What did you do to accomplish what you did? In each of the seven paragraphs, circle the one word that best describes what made the experience meaningful to you. Then sort the seven cards in order from most to least important.

2. Write a statement about yourself using each of the seven words you circled. Do this any way you like; using complete sentences is not important and it need not make sense to anyone but yourself. Example: "My achievements seemed to point out that I'm good at *trouble-shooting* problems, *organizing* meetings, *brainstorming* solutions, *summarizing* ideas, and *writing* reports."

SESSION 4:
BELIEVE YOU CAN FULFILL YOUR DESTINY

George Bernard Shaw said, "This is the true joy in life. . . . The being thoroughly worn out before you are thrown on the scrap heap.

The being a force of nature instead of a feverish, selfish, little clod of ailments."

He wanted his life to count. He wanted to be a force of nature.

Are you being a force for good? If you remember that you are special and that you can make a difference, then you can conquer the barriers in your life and get to the job of fulfilling your destiny. You do have a destiny to fulfill. How do you find it? Through reflecting, praying, and reading the Bible and other great works, you can learn how to find the right plan for your life for achieving personal significance. Just as each one of us is fashioned uniquely, we have equally unique destinies. Once you realize what your destiny is and decide to strive for it, your life will become a joy. Then you will be able to appreciate even tough times because you see them as a means for growth and significance.

Putting This to Work

These questions will help you understand your destiny.

 1. Son, what do you want to be when you grow up? Dad, what did you want to be when you grew up (when you were your son's age)?

✎   2.   Answer the following questions with your first thoughts.

- I feel most creative when . . .

- Three skills that I have mastered are . . .

1. _____

_____

2. _____

_____

3. _____

_____

- Three skills that I would like to master are . . .

1. _____

_____

2. _____

_____

3. _____

_____

- I find the greatest joy when I . . .

_____

- My idea of the greatest fun is . . .

_____

- My worst habit is . . .

_____

- This is what I believe about my ability to change:

  _____

- I am motivated by these things:

  _____

- I am concerned about these injustices which I see in the world around me:

  _____

- I do not want to have this undone at the end of my life:

  _____

- This is what I believe I ought to do with my life, what I see as my destiny:

  _____

☞ 3. Discuss your answers to the questions above. What did you learn about yourself and your dad/son? What areas would you like to change? How can your dad/son help you change these areas?

SESSION 5:
ADMIT YOUR SOFT SPOTS

Some years ago when Ron was the president of a graduate school, one of his students wanted to go out for lunch. During lunch the student said, "You are a great leader and I admire you so much."

Ron picked up the bill and paid for lunch.

Then the young man said, "Can I tell you something else that is kind of personal?"

Ron, preparing himself for an onslaught of compliments, said, "You bet!"

The student offered, "There are two things in your life about which I believe you are unaware that I believe impede your effectiveness!"

"Say what?" Ron responded.

The student repeated himself.

Now Ron was really hacked off and thought, *Who does this guy think he is—telling me that I need to work on some things in my life?* And, as Ron was leaning forward to give this guy the benefit of his wisdom, it was as though the hand of God grabbed Ron by the back of the neck and said, "Hey, Jenson. Why are you so surprised that someone should see something in your life with which you need to deal? Imagine if he saw everything I see?"

Ouch, that's a good point! thought Ron.

Isn't it amazing how defensive we can get when it comes to our weaknesses or soft spots? Fathers, if you asked your sons to write down a list of their weaknesses, or soft spots, they would need a good electric pencil sharpener nearby. The same would happen, sons, if you asked your dads to do compose a list of their shortcomings. If one of you could not think of a thing, then he would have to work on his humility. Weaknesses and shortcomings are normal and human. This is not a qualifying statement to give anyone an excuse for messing up. Rather, it is important to recognize that you have soft spots and to confront them. Running away from them is not the answer. You have to face them directly.

This seems pretty simple. But in reality it can be the hardest thing you have to do in your life because it means admitting that you are helpless. "But, but, but . . . I'm not helpless. I'm perfectly in control of my life," you might sputter. If you really are perfectly in control of your life, you would have no problem being completely honest with yourself and your friends concerning your shortcomings.

For some reason or another, many guys feel they need to be perceived as indestructible and untouchable. "We don't have any problems. We're strong. We're confident. We're men!" Bull! Guys are basically insecure creatures who want to be in control.

From our observations, the only way to be in control is to attain a true self-image. This involves admitting your soft spots. It is impossible to attain personal significance without taking an honest inventory of your strengths and weaknesses.

Putting This to Work

1. Complete the following statements.

    Dad's three biggest growth opportunities (weaknesses) as perceived by himself are:

    1. _____

    _____

    2. _____

    _____

    3. _____

    _____

    Son's three biggest growth opportunities (weaknesses) as perceived by himself are:

    1. _____

    _____

2. _____

_____

3. _____

_____

Dad's three biggest growth opportunities (weaknesses) as perceived by Son are:

1. _____

_____

2. _____

_____

3. _____

_____

Son's three biggest growth opportunities (weaknesses) as perceived by Dad are:

1. _____

_____

2. _____

_____

3. _____

_____

☞   2. Discuss when and how each of you sees these soft spots in yourself and each other. Share your insights. What one thing can you do to be more open to admitting your weaknesses? Write it down and then practice it daily. Remember it takes at least twenty-one days of continuous practice to develop a solid habit. Keep encouraging one another. List your action steps here:

To be more open to admitting my weaknesses, I will . . .

_____

_____

Day	How I practiced the new habit
1	_____
2	_____
3	_____
4	_____
5	_____
6	_____
7	_____
8	_____
9	_____
10	_____
11	_____
12	_____

13   _____

14   _____

15   _____

16   _____

17   _____

18   _____

19   _____

20   _____

21   _____

SESSION 6:
LOOK FOR OPPORTUNITIES TO GROW

Along with admitting your soft spots comes the need for a change of behavior and attitude in relation to the particular weakness. This is not easy. Both of us know that we are far too weak to keep improving on our own without backsliding. So we both have accountability groups, or small, select groups of close friends who let us know about our soft spots.

We like to pick three to five of our biggest struggles and say to one of the people in the group, "I'm struggling in these areas. Please ask me these specific questions regarding them." If one of us is having a problem telling the truth, then someone else might say, "When did you last tell a lie?" Here is a specific question that demands a specific answer.

A lot of times we beat ourselves over the head because we are not living up to our own expectations or the expectations that someone else is placing on us. We view our strengths and weaknesses in the wrong light. We need to be able to correctly identify both, to harness our strengths and work on eliminating our weaknesses.

Ron always defines an obvious weakness as a "blind spot." On occasion, he has pointed out an inappropriate behavior in Matt, saying, "I think that's a blind spot in your life." Matt typically responds, "I don't see that as a weakness!" Do you see why Ron called it a "blind" spot? Since Matt cannot recognize the fault, Ron points it out. As fathers and sons, we must take an attitude of *constructive* criticism—helping our father/son see his weaknesses.

We took this a step further and developed a system of accountability in our relationship. After recognizing our own weaknesses, we pledged to hold each other accountable by asking each other questions about progress with our soft spots. Much motivation to change comes from a network of support and honesty.

We recommend that a father and son establish an accountability relationship. There are very few ways to bond like accountability. Accountability also forces you to stay on task. When you tell your father/son about the intimate details in your life, you can get to know your father/son better and help him become a better person.

Matt and three of his friends started an accountability group that meets at a local restaurant. One of the guys said in regard to one of his soft spots, "Things were a lot easier this week because I kept thinking of you guys. It's good to know that I'm not alone in all this." What a support system! It's great to have a group of guys who are committed to helping each other grow into men with personal significance.

Putting This to Work

✎ 1. Write down the three biggest struggles in your life right now. These may include weaknesses, challenges, temptations, or questions.

1. _____

_____

2. _____

_____

3. _____

_____

☞ 2. In your time together, read your list to your dad/son, and give him permission to ask you about it in the days to come. Figure out specific questions that will enable you to pinpoint the progress of the struggle.

☞ 3. When was the last time you were caught doing something wrong? Did getting caught keep you from doing it again? You don't need to write this down. Just discuss it.

✓ 4. Identify one thing you can do this week to seek out opportunities to grow (e.g., ask your dad/son to point out areas that need work). Keep a record of what you are learning in a log.

This week I will . . .

_____

_____

_____

Day	What I learned
1	_____
2	_____
3	_____
4	_____
5	_____
6	_____
7	_____

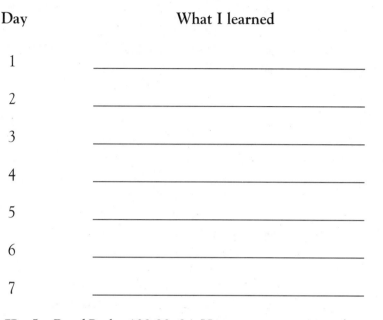

📖 5. Read Psalm 139:23–24. How can you practice this prayer in
your life?

SESSION 7:
KEEP ADJUSTING

When was the last time you failed? How did it make you feel?
How did you react? Be honest.

Well, join the club. We all fail. We are going to fail again, but
that's OK. You are not personally a failure just because you failed. A
person becomes a failure when he refuses to learn from his failures.

After each failure, you simply need to say, "I made a mistake.
That's OK. How can I learn from the situation?" Then you can focus
your eyes ahead and not look back. Remember, the goal of life is not
some pretended form of perfection. The goal of life is steady progression toward being our very best, taking things one step at a time.

Consider the track record of the following leader:

1831–Failed in business

1832–Defeated for legislature

1833–Second failure in business

1836–Suffered nervous breakdown

1838–Defeated for speaker

1840–Defeated for elector

1843–Defeated for Congress

1848–Defeated for Congress

1855–Defeated for Senate

1856–Defeated for vice president

1858–Defeated for Senate

1860–Elected President of the United States

The power of failure is what you learn as a result of failing. Abraham Lincoln learned from his failures and became one of America's most effective and beloved leaders. Do you keep growing by adjusting or do you just give up? The key to all of this is to *fall forward*. That means learn from your experience, write down your insights, and get better, not bitter.

Putting This to Work

1. List the three biggest failures you have experienced in the past year. How did you feel? What did you learn?

Failure **Lesson Learned**

1. _____

_____

2. _____

_____

3. _____

_____

☞ 2. Share your list of failures and any insights. Then examine
        Abraham Lincoln's list of failures. When might you have
        quit if you had been in his place? Why do you believe he
        did not?

☞ 3. Take this simple test for evaluating the degree of your per-
        severance. First, select a particular day; for example, yester-
        day. Second, read the statements below and disregard any
        which do not apply. Third, answer the remaining items *yes*
        or *no*, and count the number of *yes* answers.

        • My first project for the day (in the office, at home, in
          school) earned my steady attention until it was com-
          pleted.   Yes   No

        • My family knows that determination and perseverance
          are qualities that have characterized my life to this day.
          Yes   No

        • Aches and pains failed to deter me in my specific duties
          for the day.   Yes   No

        • While sentiment might have led me to relax discipline
          in my own life as well as toward my loved ones, I perse-
          vered in what seemed right to me.   Yes   No

        • Although at times I was disillusioned by others and
          tempted to withdraw from such wholesome activities as
          church boards and PTA, I continued to participate.
          Yes   No

        • Encouragement in my chosen line of endeavor was
          clearly lacking today, but I persisted in doing that which
          I felt to be right.   Yes   No

        • Nothing deterred me from pursuing all of the details rel-
          ative to my rightful duties for this day.   Yes   No

- Despite a lack of genuine desire to continue my personal reading and reflection, I stuck with it in the certain knowledge that it was the right thing to do.   Yes   No

- Today, I have kept in mind those deep, healthy desires which I know to be the ones that cultivate the principle roots in my life.   Yes   No

How well did you do? The more *yes* answers you had, the better. Share your insights.

✓ 4. From what you just learned, what one thing can you do for the next seven days to better adjust to and not give up on an issue in your life? Write it down, share it with each other, and practice it every day. Report to each other daily.

My Issue:

_____

_____

_____

_____

_____

_____

_____

To better adjust to and not give up on this issue, I will . . .

_____

_____

_____

_____

_____

_____

_____

_____

Day   **What I did**

1   _____

2   _____

3   _____

4   _____

5   _____

6   _____

7   _____

📖 5. Read Philippians 3:12–14. How did Paul keep adjusting?
        What does that mean for you?

FINAL PROJECT:
ACHIEVE PERSONAL SIGNIFICANCE

Each day, find one positive quality about your father/son, write it down, and communicate it to him in diverse and creative ways.

Day	Quality	How I communicated it to him
1	_____	_____
2	_____	_____
3	_____	_____
4	_____	_____
5	_____	_____
6	_____	_____
7	_____	_____
8	_____	_____
9	_____	_____
10	_____	_____
11	_____	_____
12	_____	_____
13	_____	_____
14	_____	_____
15	_____	_____
16	_____	_____
17	_____	_____
18	_____	_____
19	_____	_____
20	_____	_____
21	_____	_____

CHAPTER FOUR

X Out the
Negatives

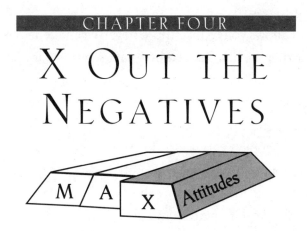

There's no getting around the fact that life has problems. As a matter of fact, we cannot change the vast majority of negative things that happen to us. But we can control how we respond to them.

Do you consider yourself an optimist or a pessimist? The difference between the two is a matter of perspective. People who are maximizing their lives are either naturally optimistic or have learned to be so. They have come to terms with the fact that while circumstances may not change, attitudes can.

This isn't to say that we should all be happy, peppy people who are always smiling no matter what. It simply means that we should cultivate a positive attitude while maintaining critical thinking skills. X-ing out the negatives does not refer to making life perfect; it means turning the negatives into positives.

This skill allows you to take those negative challenges in your life and, rather than be discouraged by them, see them as opportunities to grow and develop.

Ron just got some feedback on a training session he recently did. Ron speaks a great deal and gets a lot of positive feedback from thousands of people every year. But this recent feedback from the training session, though kind, was not the your-training-was-great kind of feedback. Instead it was the boy-do-you-need-to-improve kind of feedback. The writer gave Ron six very specific things to work on to improve the training.

Who does he think he *is?* was Ron's initial reaction to the letter. Then he reflected and allowed that the person's criticism was genuinely constructive in improving his training. So instead of being angry or hurt, Ron embraced this problem, got a positive attitude about it, and decided to put his emotional energy into learning everything he could from this constructive criticism.

Three specific skills can help you become a real craftsman in X-ing out the negatives: accepting problems, believing the best, and casting off the negatives—also known as the ABCs of right attitudes:

Accept Problems
Believe the Best
Cast Off the Negatives

Session 1:
Accept Problems

"Life is difficult" is the first sentence in Scott Peck's *The Road Less Traveled*. He states that the minute we accept life as full of pain as well as joy, we will find the fact that life is difficult to be no longer a problem. We can learn from the strug-

gles when we discover that "it is in this whole process of meeting and solving problems that life has its meaning." He goes on to say that "problems are the cutting edge that distinguishes between success and failure. . . . It is only because of problems that we grow mentally and spiritually." [1]

In short, refusing to accept problems is refusing to accept half of your life. We can guarantee you that without the problems, the good things in life seem much less impressive. What makes success so sweet is the contrast between it and failure. If we were always happy, we would be numb with it—the happiness would mean nothing. Problems give definition to the happy times in life. Accepting problems allows us to experience a fuller, richer life. How do we accept problems? First, choose joy. Notice that the phrase here is not "choose happiness." Happiness is an emotion dependent upon the circumstances. If circumstances are good, you're happy; if they're bad, you're not. Joy, on the other hand, can be present at all times. Joy is that sustaining sense of inner peace, stability, and hope that things will work out. According to Tim Hansel, "You and I were created for joy and if we miss it, we miss the reason for our existence. If our joy is honest joy, it must somehow be congruous with human tragedy. This is the test of joy's integrity. It is compatible with pain. Only the heart that hurts has a right to joy."

In the New Testament Book of James there is a passage of great insight: "When various trials and tribulations crowd into your life, don't treat them as intruders but welcome them as friends!" (James 1:2, Phillips)

Now think about that for a moment. Isn't that an irrational outlook? You are having a terrible day loaded with problems. You are sick, you are out of money, one of your friends has just rejected you, and so on. This verse says don't react to these problems as though they were intruders. How do you handle intruders? You kick them out. You try to get away from them. In some situations, you might even try to shoot them. Instead James's counsel is to welcome intruders as friends. How do you treat your friends? You try to be with them. You may even embrace them. That is what we do with our friends.

The point is you need to embrace your problems as friends. Don't react negatively to them. Embrace them.

Why? Because as you learn to embrace or choose joy in the midst of your problems, then you are able to find fulfillment, joy, and peace in the midst of circumstance. That results in contentment and completeness. And isn't that exactly what you want?

James goes on to say "the testing of your faith develops perseverance. Perseverance must finish its work so that you may be mature and complete, not lacking anything" (James 1: 3–4)

Wouldn't you like to be "mature and complete, not lacking anything"? Then choose joy.

The next time a problem enters your life (probably sometime today) embrace it. Don't react. Don't get upset, worried, or frustrated, but ask yourself, "What can I learn from this and how can I treat this as a friend?" Then utter a prayer like this, "Thank you, God, for allowing me to trust in your goodness to work this out for good in my life." Hey, even if you don't have a spiritual background, give this a try.

Second, learn from mistakes. After all, if we don't admit our mistakes, we don't grow and progress. Think of it this way: a mistake does not signify failure. Failure only comes when we refuse to recognize, admit, and learn from our mistakes. Learn to X out the negatives and make them positives.

Putting This to Work

1. List all the difficulties and challenges you faced in the last week.

   _____

   _____

   _____

   _____

   _____

   _____

   _____

2. Discuss your lists. Then take the biggest struggle you faced this week and answer these questions about it. Feel free to help each other out if this is a hard exercise.

   • What did you learn from the situation?

   • Did you "choose joy"? Did you really believe that the situation would work out for good?

   • Did the challenge create in you a fear of future failure?

📖 3. Read James 1:2–4. What is his advice? What is the benefit
     of his advice?

SESSION 2:
BELIEVE THE BEST

What you believe about something or someone
will absolutely dictate how you act around them.
Therefore, you have to take control of your
thought patterns. Believing the best is vital when
you think about others and your own life.

The way you see other people will dramatically affect how you
respond to them. Be careful not to think the worst about others.
Give them the benefit of the doubt.

In the book *Make a Life, Not Just a Living,* I (Ron) tell a story that
drove home this point to me.

> I remember some years ago showing up at the house of
> a friend of mine. I was supposed to bring some chairs. I
> rang the doorbell and he opened it and said to me, "Ron,
> where are the chairs?"
>
> I responded, "Oh I forgot." And then he glared into my
> eyes and barked out, "That figures!"
>
> I thought, *That figures? He thinks I'm no good. He thinks
> I can't follow through. He thinks I'm useless.* Then I
> thought, *Who does he think he is? The creep. I bet he's got a
> problem or twelve!*
>
> But then I decided I had one of two options. Either I
> had to believe the best about what he was saying—
> although that was pretty tough—and just forget it, or I
> had to ask him what he meant, and it was obvious to me
> what he meant.

Out of cowardice I tried to believe the best. Then a couple of weeks later I saw him again and decided to question him on the event. I asked, "You know the other day when I was at your house and forgot to bring the chairs and you said, 'That figures'?"

He interrupted me and said, "I shouldn't have said that." And I responded, "I was wondering what you meant."

He said, "Well all day long that day in every meeting someone had forgotten something. It just figured."

So, he wasn't saying, "Jenson, you're a jerk." He was saying, "My day's been terrible."

The next time you find yourself wondering what someone means when he says or does something questionable, try approaching him with something like this, "When you said [whatever it is he said] the other day, what did you mean?" You'll be amazed how many times you misread the situation.

Another way to experience joy is through thankfulness. An attitude of gratitude and appreciation is imperative in believing the best about life. All of us have countless things for which to be grateful. And when we express our thankfulness to others for what they do for us, we treat them with respect and love, and thereby enable them to feel better about themselves. Thus, you help them become the best that you believe them to be.

Putting This to Work

1. Read Philippians 4:8. How does this verse encourage you to believe the best?

✎ 2. Make a list of twenty things for which you're thankful.

1. _____   11. _____

2. _____   12. _____

3. _____   13. _____

4. _____   14. _____

5. _____   15. _____

6. _____   16. _____

7. _____   17. _____

8. _____   18. _____

9. _____   19. _____

10. _____   20. _____

☞ 3. Share your list with each other. Then come up with three ways you can demonstrate thankfulness and gratitude to each other and the other members in your family this week.

1. _____

_____

2. _____

_____

3. _____

_____

✓ 4. Commit together to practice at least one of these ways every day this week. Hold each other accountable.

SESSION 3:
CAST OFF THE NEGATIVES

When Ron was in high school, he was rather nervous about singing alone in public. Once after he sang in the cafeteria, a friend of his rushed up to see him. Ron thought that his friend was going to congratulate him, but instead his friend blurted out, "Ron, you were so-o-o-o-o flat!" Ron was very embarrassed, and he attached so much pain to singing in public that the fear of it dogged him for years.

It's not wrong to have negatives in your life. But you must learn how to cast off the inappropriate fears. Some fears are healthy and very important. For instance, you should appropriately fear breaking the law of not drinking alcoholic beverages  and driving since breaking that law could have devastating results in your life and the lives of others. However, inappropriate fears can immobilize you. In this session you will learn to reject fears, root out doubts, and realize your possibilities.

First, you must learn how to reject your fears. You can do this most effectively by changing your thinking about these fears. Instead of attaching pain or agony to a certain thought or situation, attach positive feelings to it. For instance, though Ron had a painful experience singing that solo in his high school days, he learned to attach positive feelings to singing—people being impacted, positive encouragement from others for his singing, the pleasure of doing something well and using his gifts. Do whatever is necessary to change your outlook on the situation. If that means thinking of your favorite joke or your favorite things, then do that.

Second, you have to deal with your doubts. We can deal with doubts by thinking positively and accurately. It's so easy to fall into the I'm-no-good.-Nobody-likes-me.-I-am-a-failure trap. Everyone is insecure and has doubts. We frequently assume things will go the wrong way and that we will fail. But if we look at these conclusions from an objective point of view, we can see that we assume failure will occur, when in fact, we often succeed, sometimes better than we expected.

Third, you need to realize your possibilities. Tim Hansel, an adventurer who has lived much of his life in extreme pain from a climbing accident, says, "Limitations are not necessarily negative. In fact, I'm beginning to believe that they can give life definition, clarity, and freedom. We are called to freedom of and in limitations—not from. Unrestricted water is swamp—because it lacks restriction, it lacks depth." If you are thinking positively and accurately about things, you will be able to realize your possibilities and move forward. It's only possible once you've X-ed out the negatives. Until this happens, though, you're stuck treading water . . . in a swamp.

Ron tells a story in his *Make a Life* book that drives this point home:

> In the 1952 Olympics, a young Hungarian boy peered down the barrel of his gun and hit the bull's-eye repeatedly. He was flawless. His perfect right hand and eye coordination won him the gold medal.
>
> Tragically, he lost his right arm six months later. But just four years after the accident, he went to the Olympic Games in Melbourne where he won his second gold medal with his left hand. He determined not to be limited by his limitations, but to see his possibilities.

Putting This to Work

1. When were you the most afraid in your life? What did you feel like? What went on in your mind?

_____

_____

_____

_____

_____

_____

_____

_____

2. In your time together identify *why* you were afraid. What kind of incorrect thinking and assumptions are attached to this fear?

3. Commit to practice "casting off the negative" every time you are confronted with it this week. Daily report to one another on how you are doing. Keep up the encouragement. Remember, you aren't a failure if you fail; you are just more seasoned and wise if you learn from this experience.

4. Read Psalm 55:22 and 1 Peter 5:7. How can you deal with your fears and worries?

FINAL PROJECT: X OUT THE NEGATIVES

Problems + Joy = Patience

Patience + Time +

Repetition =

Completeness

Identify a major challenge or problem you are facing right now and write it down here and on a 3" x 5" card. Write the above equation on the other side of the card. Every time you face this concern, decide to "choose joy" by the following means:

- Accepting the fact that it will work out if you work in right principles.

- Writing down ways that you are growing personally because of this issue.

Then practice, practice, practice the preceding two steps for twenty-one days.

Day	Practice
1	_____
2	_____
3	_____
4	_____
5	_____
6	_____
7	_____
8	_____
9	_____
10	_____
11	_____
12	_____
13	_____
14	_____
15	_____
16	_____
17	_____
18	_____
19	_____
20	_____
21	_____

CHAPTER FIVE

INTERNALIZE RIGHT PRINCIPLES

"What's the right thing to do in this situa-tion?" Have you ever asked yourself that question? Sure you have, just as we have. The big issue is *how* you decide the right thing to do. The key is to know what is right. So how do you know what is right? What are the non-negotiable principles that govern your life?

Our society has seen an unbelievable decline in its ethical standards and morals in recent years. Americans in general have accepted a watered-down alternative to abso-lute principles and have distorted values. You can see for yourself how bad things are.

People are shot for their designer shoes, kids sue their parents, and many churches fall apart because of immorality. People are too concerned with not offending anybody and being as politically correct as possible. But this leaves people with no clear, unchanging standard to judge their words and actions. If we want to do what we think is good and right, how do we figure out what *good and right* is?

That's the purpose of the fourth principle of MAXIMIZERS: Internalize right principles. It will help you determine your own code of ethics, decide what improvements you should make, and build them into your life.

This chapter will discuss the V.A.L.U.E.S. acrostic:

Verify your own values.

Articulate your philosophy.

Learn the right perspective on issues.

Unpack right values through action.

Evaluate your growth.

Share your values with others.

SESSION 1:
VERIFY YOUR OWN VALUES

To integrate right principles, you must first verify your own values. What's important to you? What occupies your thinking? What could you not do without in life? Who are your heroes?

Now, when we ask you what your values are, we don't mean the values you wish you had or the values you think you should have. If you want to internalize right principles, you have to start with a fair inventory of what your values are right now. Be honest so you will know which values you're satisfied with and which ones you think could use some improvement.

Understanding your own values is important because your values dictate your actions, and your actions have an impact on others. Consider what columnist Jack Griffin says in his article "It's OK, Son, Everybody Does It," printed in the *Chicago Sun Times* years ago:

When Johnny was six years old, he was with his father when they were caught speeding. His father handed the officer a twenty dollar bill with his driver's license. "It's OK, son," his father said as they drove off. "Everybody does it."

When he was eight, he was present at a family council presided over by Uncle George, on the surest means to shave points off the income tax return. "It's OK, kid," his uncle said. "Everybody does it."

When he was nine, his mother took him to his first theater production. The box office man couldn't find any seats until his mother discovered an extra $5 in her purse. "It's OK, son," she said. "Everybody does it."

When he was twelve, he broke his glasses on the way to school. His Aunt Francine persuaded the insurance company that they had been stolen and they collected $75. "It's OK, kid," she said. "Everybody does it."

When he was fifteen, he made right guard on the high school football team. His coach showed him how to block and at the same time grab the opposing end by the shirt so the official couldn't see it. "It's OK, kid," the coach said. "Everybody does it."

When he was sixteen, he took his first summer job at the supermarket. His assignment was to put the overripe strawberries in the bottom of the boxes and the good ones on top where they would show. "It's OK, kid," the manager said. "Everybody does it."

When he was eighteen, Johnny and a neighbor applied for a college scholarship. Johnny was a marginal student. His neighbor was in the upper 3 percent of his class, but he couldn't play right guard. Johnny got the scholarship. "It's OK, son," his parents said. "Everybody does it."

When he was nineteen, he was approached by an upperclassman who offered the test answers for $50. "It's OK, kid," he said. "Everybody does it."

Johnny was caught and sent home in disgrace. "How could you do this to your mother and me?" his father said. "You never learned anything like this at home." His aunt and uncle were also shocked. If there's one thing the adult world can't stand, it's a kid who cheats.[1]

What kind of model are you, Dad? How about you, Son?

Putting This to Work

1. Look at a news magazine (*Time, Newsweek*, etc.) and identify what values are reflected in three advertisements (money, sex, popularity, family, etc.).

2. What three things do you value most (something you own, something you like to do, something you cherish)?

1. _____

   _____

2. _____

   _____

3. _____

   _____

✎   3. Evaluate your own values by answering these questions:

   • How do you spend your time?

   _____

   _____

   _____

   • How do you spend your money?

   _____

   _____

   _____

   • Who are your heroes?

   _____

   _____

   _____

   • What do you think about most when you're alone?

   _____

   _____

   _____

☞   4. Discuss how you have answered the previous questions. Help each other realize that these are what each of you values. What surprises you most about your values?

📖   5. Read Philippians 1:9–11. How important is it to discern your values?

SESSION 2:
ARTICULATE YOUR PHILOSOPHY

Once you have verified your own values, you can articulate your philosophy of life, that is, how you view life and how you should live it. What is important to you? How do you see things? If you do not have concrete values and a firm philosophy, then the culture and environment around you will determine those for you. Let's be brutally honest: either you identify and articulate the values you want for yourself, or you can expect to spend the rest of your life as a slave to what other people, your own problems, cultural pressures, and impure, bad habits impose on you. The choice is yours.

One good example of a life philosophy and core set of principles is the Boy Scout Oath: "On my honor, I will do my best: To do my duty to God and my country, and to obey the Scout Law; to help other people at all times; to keep myself physically strong, mentally awake, and morally straight."

Another great set of core values is the Ten Commandments. Here they are in a modern version:

1. Never worship any god but Me.

2. Never make idols; don't worship images.

3. Use My name when you are calling on Me or talking about Me; not for irresponsible exclamations.

4. Keep the Sabbath day holy.

5. Honor your father and mother.

6. You must not murder.

7. You must not commit adultery.

8. You must not steal.

9. You must not tell lies.

10. You must not burn with desire for another person's spouse, nor envy him for his home, land, nor anything else he owns.

Consider a portion of ABC TV anchorman Ted Koppel's commencement address to Duke University seniors in May of 1987:

We have actually convinced ourselves that slogans will save us. "Shoot up if you must, but use a clean needle." "Enjoy sex whenever and with whomever you wish, but wear a condom."

No. The answer is no. Not no because it isn't cool . . . or smart . . . or because you might end up in jail or dying in an AIDS ward—but no . . . because it's wrong. Because we have spent five thousand years as a race of rational human beings trying to drag ourselves out of the primeval slime by searching for truth . . . and moral absolutes.

In the place of Truth we have discovered facts; for moral absolutes we have substituted moral ambiguity. We now communicate with everyone . . . and say absolutely nothing. We have reconstructed the Tower of Babel and it is a television antenna. A thousand voices producing a daily parody of democracy; in which everyone's opinion is afforded equal weight; regardless of substance or merit. Indeed, it can even be argued that opinions of real weight tend to sink with barely a trace in television's ocean of banalities.

Our society finds Truth too strong a medicine to digest undiluted. In its purest form Truth is not a polite tap on the shoulder; it is a howling reproach.

What Moses brought down from Mount Sinai were not the Ten Suggestions . . . they are Commandments. Are, not were.

The sheer brilliance of the Ten Commandments is that they codify, in a handful of words, acceptable human behavior. Not just for then . . . or now . . . but for all time. Language evolves . . . power shifts from nation to nation. Man erases one frontier after another; and yet we and our behavior . . . and the Commandments which govern that behavior . . . remain the same.

I caution you, as one who performs daily on that flickering altar, to set your sights beyond what you can see. There is true majesty in the concept of an unseen power which can neither be measured nor weighed. There is harmony and inner peace to be found in following a moral compass that points in the same direction, regardless of fashion or trend.

This is a pretty good starting place for building your own straight lines.

Putting This to Work

☞ 1. What three things would you like to be most important in your life? Share these with one another. Reread the Boy Scout Oath and circle those words or ideas that you would like to be true of your own life. Discuss why they are important to you.

✎ 2. List at least one principle or aspect you value in each of the following areas:

   • Faith (e.g., seek to honor God always)

   _____

   _____

   _____

- Fitness (e.g., take care of my body)

_____

_____

_____

- Family (e.g., love my family and put their needs before those of other relationships)

_____

_____

_____

- Friends

_____

_____

_____

- Firm/business/school

_____

_____

_____

- Finances

_____

_____

_____

- Favor

_____

_____

_____

From this list develop a clear statement of what is important to you.

_____

_____

_____

☞ 3. Discuss your list and your values statement with your dad/
        son.

📖 4. Read Hebrews 5:11–14. How can you prepare yourself for
        "solid food"?

SESSION 3:
LEARN THE RIGHT PERSPECTIVE ON ISSUES

Socrates said, "You never know a line is crooked unless you have
a straight one to put next to it." Pretty good words. If you don't look
at life from the right perspective, then you won't see the crooked
nature of it. You learn the right perspective on issues when you realize that there are absolutes and then strive to understand and follow
them.

Think for a moment about how you learned to do the right thing.
Start with your family and your upbringing. How did that help you?
I (Ron) grew up in a warm and friendly atmosphere. My mother and
father were hardworking, kind, ethical people. Learning hard work,

honesty, commitment, thriftiness, and other values from my parents helped me build a solid foundation of knowing what is right.

As I moved into my junior high years, I had a spiritual transformation. I came to believe in Christ. Following this experience, I read the Bible and prayed, developing a deeper understanding about what I ought and ought not to do to live a life pleasing to my Savior.

Also, I had many mentors and encouragers in my life who gave me direction and support. These people helped to teach me about living a life that honors God and others. Much of my support has also come from good books and audiotapes.

What about you?

Putting This to Work

1. What are some specific ways you learn the right perspective on issues? Who do you measure yourself and your ideas against?

_____

_____

2. What are the movies or TV shows that have influenced you?

_____

_____

3. Who are the people that serve as your guides of right and wrong?

_____

_____

✎ 4. What impact has your spiritual life and religious community had on your life principles? Where will you go in the future for direction in this area? How will you begin? What will you do?

_____

_____

📖 5. Read Romans 12:1–2. How can you find out what God considers right and wrong?

SESSION 4:
UNPACK RIGHT VALUES THROUGH ACTION

Now comes the fun part—and the hard work. But remember, as we discussed in chapter 2, "Make Things Happen," hard work can be energizing and worthwhile when it is focused on accomplishing something significant and valuable. Our focus in this session is to internalize right principles, moving from theory to action.

After establishing values and life philosophies, you are ready to put them to work. You can do this in your personal, family, or business/school lives. First, burn that value into your mind. Meditate about it many times in the day. Think about ways you can apply the value. Be really specific. Think of people you see frequently—teachers, students, coworkers, or family members—and apply the principle in your relationships with them. In your weekly planners, schedule the specific activities that you've listed for building this principle into your life. Then do them.

Putting This to Work

📖 1. Read James 1:22–25. How vital is practicing the truth rather than just knowing it?

📖 2. This week, buy or borrow *The Book of Virtues* by William Bennett. Read it (it is filled with resources to help you learn the right perspective on issues).

✎ 3. Write the MAXIMIZERS Creed on a 3" x 5" card.

MAXIMIZERS Creed

I Will Take Charge of My Life and Make a Difference
I Will Live My Life with a Sense of Dignity
I Will Embrace Problems as Positive Opportunities
I Will Center My Life on Universal Principles
I Will Passionately Pursue My Mission
I Will Keep All Vital Areas of My Life in Balance
I Will Put Others First and Honestly Serve Them
I Will Cultivate My Character and Spirit
I Will Keep Adjusting to Needs
I Will Never, Ever, Ever Quit

Now, take five minutes right now and memorize this creed. Go ahead. Memorize it! Then say it to each other. Go ahead, you can do it! And coach one another with the right phrases as you do this.

Take a few minutes and brainstorm how you could put this creed to work this week. For example, you might practice taking charge of your life by being disciplined in your father-son study times together. Why don't you write your next meeting time together in your schedule?

Read—or better yet, say from memory—the MAXIMIZERS Creed at least four times a day this week (breakfast, lunch, dinner, bedtime). Each time, think long and hard about these principles and their application in life.

SESSION 5:
EVALUATE YOUR GROWTH

Some years ago, Ron was teaching a group of leaders to build goals in their lives. He suggested that they all write specific, measurable goals and hold each other accountable to them. Before he could finish, one of the newer guys—let's call him "Mr. Helpful"—said, "Great! What's one of your goals?" Being on the spot, Ron had to come up with a goal, so he said, "To lose twenty pounds."

"Terrific," Mr. Helpful said. "I'll bring a scale here every week and then you can stand on it and we'll see how well you are doing."

Ron shuddered at the thought and tried to get out of the arrangement but had no luck. So every week Mr. Helpful brought the scale, and Ron was held accountable for losing weight. He did all right for a while, but then one week he just pigged out. He knew he had not only not lost weight but gained some. Fearing the meeting that week, Ron was relieved when Mr. Helpful showed up without his scale.

Ron told the group that it was no problem. He would go upstairs to his scale, weigh himself, and then tell them the results. Well, Mr. Helpful would have none of that: he made Ron go up and get the scale and bring it down to the meeting . . . which Ron did.

Holding yourself and others accountable in doing what you say you are going to do is important. It may seem hard, but it is a key element in bringing about real, lasting change in our lives.

The fact of the matter is that we can't make it on our own. There are too many temptations and roadblocks to success without loving, caring (and nonjudgmental) support. A father-and-son relationship can be extremely meaningful if you will simply commit to love and support each other.

You can start by helping each other in the following area of evaluation.

If you want to internalize right principles, you need to know what kind of progress you're making on the way. You can do this by regularly and consistently evaluating your growth. So for one week, take time at the end of each day to ask the following questions related to your stated values:

1. Did I schedule my right principles and philosophy into my daily life/calendar?

2. Did I keep my schedule as I planned?

3. How did I spend my free time?

4. Where did I spend my money?

5. What did I daydream or dwell upon?

6. Did my values inside match my values outside?

Along with these questions, it's often beneficial to join or establish some type of support group or accountability group. We'll talk more about accountability later in the book because this is an incredible way to become genuine and honest with yourself.

SESSION 6:
SHARE THESE TRUTHS WITH OTHERS

Sharing these truths (those principles you wrote down in session 2 of this chapter) with others does not mean being pushy or obnoxious. You can communicate by being formative or reformative. Formative communication includes forming (or building) these principles into people's lives by talking about them and by living them out in your life. The second method of communication, reformative communication, deals with helping people get back on track when they have violated one of these principles. Reforming means forming again, and that's what reformative communication does.

Whether it's through formative or reformative communication, there are four aspects of effective communication that help you engage your audience. First, be sure to communicate with people genuinely and at their level. If you don't, then your listeners will have no desire to claim the truths you have claimed.

Second, communicate positively and specifically. Dad, if you think your son has a problem with lying, don't say, "You've got all sorts of problems, but I only have time to work on the lying right now." Instead, say something like, "You know, Son, there are many qualities in your life that I wish I had. However, I think there's one area in your life where you may need some improvement." Which way of communicating do you think is more effective?

Third, communicate practically. People need practical methods to build these absolute principles into their lives. Give your listeners realistic, attainable steps for growth.

Fourth, communicate patiently and kindly. Some people may not like what you say and some may not listen at all, but if you betray any impatience or anger, you lose your credibility and impact. Remember, putting truth in people's hearts requires an appealing presentation, so when you give the gift of truth, wrap the package with sincerity, kindness, patience, and practicality.

Basically, be a champion for values. Don't be part of the majority who are afraid to talk about the truth. Don't leave a legacy of wishy-washy relativism behind you. Leave a legacy of values, of truth, of right. It's your choice.

Putting This to Work

✎   1. Take the next few minutes to write down one principle/
        value that's really important to you. Perhaps because you
        value people, the principle is being kind to someone.

        _____

        _____

        _____

        _____

        _____

☞   2. Imagine that your father/son is not being kind to other peo-
        ple. Act out how you would communicate this principle of
        being kind to others with your unkind father/son. Be sure to
        communicate personally, positively, practically and
        patiently.

        When you're done, evaluate your performance. Write
        down your mistakes.

        _____

        _____

        _____

        _____

        _____

        _____

FINAL PROJECT:
INTERNALIZE RIGHT PRINCIPLES

For the next twenty-one days, practice the following two assignments. Remember, you must build straight lines into your life. It's like having "true north" principles to guide you. Just as the magnetic north pole gives clarity to our direction physically, these universal principles (MAXIMIZERS and others) give clarity to our personal direction.

    1. Keep a daily log of the values communicated through discussions, TV shows, advertisements, conversations, and so forth. Share nightly what you're learning with your father/son.

Day   **Values from TV, ads, conversations, etc.**

1   _____

2   _____

3   _____

4   _____

5   _____

6   _____

7   _____

8   _____

9   _____

10   _____

11 _____

12 _____

13 _____

14 _____

15 _____

16 _____

17 _____

18 _____

19 _____

20 _____

21 _____

2. Write down the Boy Scout Oath on a 3" x 5" card. Dwell on this concept four times a day (breakfast, lunch, dinner, and bedtime). Keep it up for twenty-one days. Track your discoveries, insights, and progress below.

Day **Discoveries, insights, progress**

1 _____

2 _____

3 _____

4 _____

5 _____

6 _____

7 _____

8 _____

9 _____

10 _____

11 _____

12 _____

13 _____

14 _____

15 _____

16 _____

17 _____

18 _____

19 _____

20 _____

21 _____

CHAPTER SIX

MARCH TO A MISSION

Have you ever played the game where you press your forehead to the tip of a baseball bat that is standing upright on the floor, and then, keeping your forehead on the tip and facing the floor, walk around the bat as fast as you can? Then you drop the bat and attempt to race to the finish line. Wow! You can barely stand up, much less get to the finish line very easily. You are so disoriented.

And you know what? That is how many of us live our lives. We don't have any clear focus. We are disoriented—stumbling through life.

Take the next few minutes to ask and answer these questions:

- Where do you see yourself in ten years?
- What are you going to be doing?
- How will you be spending your time?

There is a real sense in which we are all still very much in process. It doesn't make much difference how old we are; we are still going somewhere.

Where are you going with your life? This is a critical question to answer. Moreover, I (Ron) have researched hundreds of leaders over the years and they have identified *having a lifelong mission* as one of the ten critical principles for successful living.

This chapter will evaluate the four aspects of the word *mission* and provide practical steps toward the achievement of your mission. We will deal with:

Purpose—Why Do I Exist?

Vision—So What That I Exist?

Roles—How Do I Fulfill My Mission?

Goals—Where and When Do I Accomplish My Mission?

March—How Do I March to This Mission?

Practice—How Do I Begin to March to This Mission?

Mission encompasses all areas as seen in this graphic.

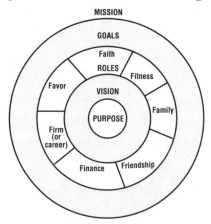

Mission is something to march to, not run through. Life is not a sprint. You're in it for the long haul, and without deliberate marching, you will get lost. And *marching* implies a stated destination. You either get where you're going or you don't. Marching also implies having a clear purpose: a battle plan. Life is a battlefield, and you've got to face it as such.

George Bernard Shaw said it this way: "This is the true joy in life, the being used for a purpose recognized by yourself as a mighty one; the being thoroughly worn out before you are thrown on the scrap heap; the being a force of Nature instead of a feverish selfish little clod of ailments and grievances complaining that the world will not devote itself to making you happy."[1]

Putting This to Work

One of our favorite personalities of all time is the apostle Paul. He began his life as a religious zealot who actually persecuted the early Christians. Then he went through a paradigm shift (that is, he began to see life in a radically different way) through a dramatic experience that lead him to become a follower of Christ.

📖 1. Read the following Bible passage several times. Underline key words and phrases that reflect the various aspects of mission as identified above. Write your insights below. After you have done this work, answer the questions that are stated below.

> Do you not know that in a race all the runners run, but only one gets the prize? Run in such a way as to get the prize. Everyone who competes in the games goes into strict training. They do it to get a crown that will not last; but we do it to get a crown that will last forever. Therefore I do not run like a

man running aimlessly; I do not fight like a man
beating the air. No, I beat my body and make it my
slave so that after I have preached to others, I
myself will not be disqualified for the prize. (1 Cor.
9:24–27)

_____

_____

_____

_____

☞   2. How does Paul view life? What is the metaphor and what
        are the implications for a mission-minded lifestyle?

☞   3. What qualities are true in Paul's life as he reaches for his
        mission?

☞   4. How should *marching to a mission* be guiding your life as a
        result of this text?

SESSION 1:
PURPOSE—WHY DO I EXIST?

Purpose answers the specific question, *Why do I exist?* The starting
point in developing your sense of mission is answering that. So, why
do you exist? What is the overarching direction of your life? Where
are you headed?

In Lewis Carroll's *Alice in Wonderland,* the cheshire cat sagely
states, "If you don't know where you are heading, any road will do."
Dads, if you want to maximize your lives and help your sons do the
same, you must work together to understand your purpose. The first
step is to assess what's truly important to you. What are your ideol-
ogies, beliefs, morals, and convictions? What would you die for and,

more important, what are you living for? It's important that you articulate your purpose in a written statement that is concise and focused to remind you of your direction in life.

Ron's purpose statement is "To know God and to make Him known."

Matt's purpose statement is "To glorify God in everything and in so doing give an accurate and dynamic account of who Christ is."

Putting This to Work

1. List three unique strengths and skills you possess that you can use to have a positive impact on the world.

   1. _____

   _____

   2. _____

   _____

   3. _____

   _____

2. Complete these statements:

   • I work best at . . .

   _____

   _____

   _____

- If I could do anything, I'd most like to . . .

  _____

  _____

  _____

  _____

  _____

- I am happiest when . . .

  _____

  _____

  _____

- Three things I would like to accomplish during my life
  are . . .

  1. _____

  2. _____

  3. _____

3. Fill in your own personal purpose statement based on your
   answers above.

   I exist to . . .

   _____

   _____

SESSION 2:
VISION—SO WHAT THAT I EXIST?

A man came into the kitchen just in time to see his wife slice off the end of a roast and put it in the roasting pan. He asked her, "Honey, why did you cut off the end of the roast?"

She said, "I don't know, I've just always done it."

"Well why?" he asked.

"I don't know, but Mom did," she answered.

"But why?"

"I don't know. We'll have to call Mom."

So she called her mother and said, "Mom, why did you always cut off the end of the roast?"

There was a pregnant pause. Mom laughed a little bit and said, "That's a good question. I do it because Grandma did."

"Why?"

"I don't know. Ask Grandma."

So they called Grandma and asked, "Grandma, why do you cut off the end of the roast?" And she said, "Because my roaster is too small."

Well, that's how many of us live. We don't do things because of a sense of direction and vision, but because we've always done it that way.

Helen Keller was once asked if she could think of anything worse than having no sight. She said, "Oh yes, what is worse is to have sight but no vision."

The second major element of mission is *vision*, which answers the question, *So what that I exist?* In other words, what will be the long-term impact of my having walked on this earth? What kind of legacy will I have left?

Having a vision statement may motivate you even more than the purpose statement because you can visualize the kind of impact you hope to have with your life. So how do you see the world being different because you existed?

Putting This to Work

1. Read Proverbs 29:18. What is life like without vision?

2. *Kapow!* You were shot in the head. Despite the doctors' efforts, you didn't pull through. But you've come back in spirit to look at your life. Ask the following questions of each other. Be honest!

   • What did you leave undone?

   • What did you always want to do that you never did?

   • What was your greatest accomplishment and why?

   • Whose lives were touched positively because of you, and how?

   • In twenty words or less, how will you be remembered by others?

3. Oops! You didn't die. We just thought you were dead. But as the doctors miraculously revived you, they discovered two fascinating things—some good news and some bad news. First, the good news: you're going to have great health the rest of your life. Now the bad news: you have exactly *ten more years* from today to live after which time your ticker will tick its last tock. Therefore, answer the same questions once more based on this new scenario.

   • What did you leave undone?

   • What did you always want to do that you never did?

- What was your greatest accomplishment and why?

- Whose lives were touched positively because of you, and how?

- In twenty words or less, how will you be remembered by others?

4. In light of your above answers, summarize how you want the world to be different because you existed. Remember, this is *your vision* of how you would like the world to be.

   As a result of my life, I envision . . .

   _____

   _____

   _____

   _____

   _____

   _____

   _____

   _____

   _____

   _____

Ron's vision statement is "a world globe reflecting bright lights in every major influence center—these indicate maximizers reflecting winning values and building these values in their families, institutions, communities and countries."

Matt's vision statement is "an American society taking a stand, morally, spiritually, relationally, and one in which people are pur-pose-driven."

SESSION 3:
ROLES—HOW DO I FULFILL MY MISSION?

The third aspect of mission is the area of roles. *Roles* answer the question, *Where is your mission accomplished?* Every one of us has multiple roles in our life. To succeed in accomplishing our mission in one or two roles and to fail in other roles ultimately results in fail-ure in life. How many of us accomplish great things in work or in school, but fail in our personal lives? Oscar Wilde said it this way:

> The gods had given me almost everything. But I let myself
> be lured into long spells of senseless and sensual ease . . . .
> Tired of being on the heights, I deliberately went to the
> depths in search for new sensation. What the paradox was
> to me in the sphere of thought, perversity became to me
> in the sphere of passion. I grew careless of the lives of oth-
> ers. I took pleasure where it pleased me, and passed on. I
> forgot that every little action of the common day makes
> or unmakes character, and that therefore what one has
> done in the secret chamber, one has some day to cry aloud
> from the housetop. I ceased to be lord over myself. I was
> no longer the captain of my soul, and did not know it. I
> allowed pleasure to dominate me. I ended in horrible dis-
> grace.[2]

How do you respond to this quotation? In what areas could you potentially fail? How can you both help one another here?

Remember, you are a whole person and your mission needs to impact all areas of your life. The beginning place in developing your roles is to identify the various aspects of your life that are important to you.

Some people break these roles down into mental, physical, emotional, and spiritual categories. Others tend to group roles under personal, business, financial, recreational, and educational areas.

In chapter 5, we examined certain roles when we looked at articulating your philosophy. Here are Ron's roles:

- Faith (relationship with God)
- Fitness (mental, emotional, physical, etc.)
- Family (wife, children, extended family)
- Friends
- Finances
- Firm (business activities including research, product development, consulting, speaking, marketing, etc.)
- Favor (giving back to people)

Most of these have subroles/subcategories. For instance, under *Firm,* which really stands for business interests, Ron has various roles.

These are Matt's roles:

- Spiritual growth
- Family growth
- Relational growth (friends, dates)
- Mental growth (school)
- Emotional growth

Putting This to Work

1. Identify what you consider to be the important roles of your life. Don't leave out any aspects of life, and remember that this is *your list*. Make it fit your style. As trite as it sounds, there's no right and wrong here. In regards to your career/school roles, make sure that they reflect your ideals, which are not necessarily what you're doing right now. You may be driving a cab right now or attending school when you would like to be working in public relations or marketing.

   Don't be afraid to dream big. If you want to make a significant impact in some venue (and we assume you do because you've taken the energy to read this book), then you need to believe that you can accomplish what you set out to do.

   _____

   _____

   _____

   _____

   _____

   _____

   _____

   _____

   _____

   _____

_____

_____

☞ 2. Imagine what you would do in an ideal week, that is, a week that would reflect your ideals. Talk about the activities you would be involved in. Then, based on your perfect week's activities, determine what your roles are.

☞ 3. Read Ephesians 5:22–6:9. How many roles are illustrated here? Note the directions that help fulfill the role.

SESSION 4: GOALS—WHERE AND WHEN DO I ACCOMPLISH MY MISSION?

The final step in developing your sense of mission is to articulate specific goals related to each role. You may have two to four goals or even more for each role, and some roles may demand more goals than others.

Goals answer the question, *How do I accomplish my mission?* In light of your purpose, vision, and roles, how do you propose to fulfill your mission? Here you must get specific; otherwise, you will have some uninspiring, unachievable, but nice ideas down in print.

The culture around us (including the media, our friends, bad habits, wrong views about life, and so on) will keep pushing us toward living a lackluster life that goes around in circles and leads to ultimate frustration and disappointment. A clear set of objectives will give you the target and momentum necessary to cast off dead weight and have a more productive, meaningful, and happy life.

For goals to work well, they need to meet the A.I.M.S. test:

Achievable. Don't set a goal so high that it cannot be reached. For instance, don't set a goal to be a concert pianist if you hate piano and do not have talent. But do stretch yourself in areas in which you feel motivated.

Inspiring. Shoot high in those areas where you have interest and desire. Ron grew up in a middle-class community where most people were content to continue living as they always had. He set goals to develop himself and that enabled him to achieve well beyond what was expected. That is true of all high achievers. They reach high toward inspiring goals.

One of the best ways to accomplish this is to articulate what will happen if you do or do not achieve each goal. For instance, if you set a goal to build a lifelong friendship with your father/ son but don't, what will the consequences be? Perhaps guilt, hurt, disappointment, regrets, bad models for grandchildren and others, disharmony in other areas of relationships, and so forth, will haunt you. But if you reach that goal, the results might be fulfillment, joy, peace, happiness, good models established for others, and so forth.

It is *critical* that you ascribe pros and cons to each objective. Without attaching pain (to not achieving the object) and pleasure (to achieving it), chances are you will not achieve the desired results. Your present momentum will just keep you going the way you are going now.

Measurable. It is one thing to move in a direction and quite another to specifically identify where you are going and what you want to achieve. You must have measurability into your goals. Answer these questions: When will I achieve this? How will I know I have achieved it? Where will this be achieved? For instance, if a life goal is to exercise, you may state it this way: Do aerobic exercise for thirty minutes four times a week.

Shared. There is a synergy in working on goals together. This MAXIMIZERS program is a great time for you and your father/son to communicate your life goals and the specific strategies you have to achieve those goals.

Here are some examples of goals with pain and pleasure attached.

Ron's personal fitness: To do aerobic exercise for thirty minutes four times a week.

- What if I don't achieve it? How will I feel? I will be sluggish, not accomplish what I could, feel poorly, get overweight, shorten my life span.

- What if I do achieve it? How will I feel? I will be at my peak, more dynamic, live longer, have richer relationships, enjoy life more, be a better example, be a real steward of this body God has given me.

Matt's mental growth: To read at least forty-five minutes day.

- What if I don't achieve it? How will I feel? I will get behind on my work, learn less than I could have, do poorer in classes, keep my brain from being sharp, attain no mental self-discipline, feel lazy.

- What if I do achieve it? How will I feel? My mind will be active, and I will enjoy learning and be learning more. I will also feel good about my self-discipline and feel better prepared for future studies and life. I will become a better critical thinker.

Putting This to Work

1. What are the top three goals you would like to have for the next twelve months? Write these down, make them specific, and share them with one another.

   1. _____

   2. _____

   3. _____

✎   2. Begin to develop goals. Using some of the roles from session 2, add at least one goal that passes the AIMS test and attach pain and pleasure to it. Using the format below, write down one goal for each of the areas listed below. Share with one another what you learn.

  • Role: (family)

  _____

  _____

  • Goal:

  _____

  _____

     What if I don't achieve it? How will I feel?

  _____

  _____

     What if I do achieve it? How will I feel?

  _____

  _____

  • Role: (profession—work/school)

  _____

  _____

  • Goal:

  _____

  _____

What if I don't achieve it? How will I feel?

_____

_____

What if I do achieve it? How will I feel?

_____

_____

✎ 3. Now that you have the idea, take some clean sheets of paper and try to write life goals for each area of your life (you may have fifteen or twenty). Be sure you cover all areas you are responsible for. By defining your goals, you are on your way to success in all areas of your life.

📖 4. Read Philippians 3:12–16. Did Paul (the author of Philippians) aim at goals? How?

SESSION 5:
MARCH—HOW DO I MARCH TO THIS MISSION?

In the last session you put your goals down on paper. But writing all of this down is just the beginning. How do we put it to work? We have found there are certain steps in this march: (1) gain information, (2) study people who model this principle, (3) put these ideas to work, and (4) evaluate routinely. We'll study the first two in this session, then the last two in the next session (session 6).

First, *gain more information*. Beyond learning about mission generically through books and tapes, Ron has helped Matt identify his strengths and weaknesses, has exposed him to inspirational people and settings (such as traveling together to Russia and Asia), and has shared his own sense of mission and goals with Matt.

Much of marching to a mission has to do with motivation. It's easy enough to define your mission statement, but it gets hard when you have to motivate yourself without anyone supporting or pushing you. Matt found a lot of incentive in reading books and listening to motivational tapes. We find that reading material by people with mission statements similar to our own helps inspire us to grow. There definitely is a power in words which gives people sufficient motivation to keep striving in their missions.

One of the best ways to focus your mission in life is through prayer. We both feel that we have been weak in this area of our lives, especially regarding praying together. And if we could do it over again, we certainly would have developed times on a weekly basis to come together and pray.

Second, *study people who have modeled healthy mission-driven lives.* We have both worked to be exposed to models of mission over the years. We have made our home a place for friends and acquaintances of all types. Many of these have been powerful leaders who have filled our home with life-changing stories from around the world.

For instance, our Australian friend, Alan, recently spent three days with us. Alan was between trips to Russia where he was putting together some very sophisticated business deals. Since it is extremely difficult to establish a business in Russia, every obstacle that could be faced was faced by Alan. But he is a man with a mission and his telling us about his struggles and victories taught us much.

I (Ron) have grown in this process by interviewing leaders around the world who reflect the MAXIMIZERS principles found in this workbook. Early in my career, my wife—Mary—and I toured the United States in a twenty-foot motor home, interviewing 350 highly respected leaders. We covered twenty thousand miles and thirty-eight states. This trip, part of my doctoral work research, was life-changing. (Of course, living with another couple in a twenty-foot motor home was also life-changing, but that's another story.)

These leaders had built great institutions from their sense of mission. They oozed mission; their mission permeated everything they did. They were gripped by a cause and they reflected it in their work, their relationships, and their corporate culture. These people were in a war to make a difference and they lived like it.

The most poignant meeting I had was with Bill Bright, the founder and president of Campus Crusade for Christ, one of the largest nonprofit organizations in the world. Do you think he senses he is marching to mission with an organization name like that?

What fascinated me most about this meeting was not the organization itself, although it was more than impressive (currently in 150+ countries, 50,000+ staff, $200+ million budget). What touched me is that when asked about his mission, Bill Bright did not mention the organization, other than to say, "God has been gracious to us." Instead he simply said, "I am a bond servant of the Lord. And my job is to love Him and tell the world about Him." Then he wept.

That experience marked me and my family for life. Here was a man who not only had a zeal for his work but a passion for his God. He truly marched to a mission!

Moreover, many of our friends reflect this type of mission-mindedness (after all, like attracts like). And we often vacation together as families. The result is that we have "caught" mission-mindedness.

Putting This to Work

☞ 1. What are things you can both do to keep growing in the area of mission? Brainstorm for ten minutes. Remember, when you brainstorm you do not evaluate. You come up with creative (even off-the-wall) ideas. After you have brainstormed, decide which ones sound the best and give them an "A" rating.

☞ 2. Identify some people whom you admire. Talk about mission mentors and develop a strategy to get to know more about them.

📖 3. Find biographies of mission-minded people. Consider reading them together and talking about the qualities of their lives that you want to emulate.

📖 4. Read Colossians 1:9–11. What roles do constant study and application play.

SESSION 6:
PRACTICE—HOW DO I BEGIN TO MARCH TO THIS MISSION?

The previous session considers the importance of growing in knowledge and studying people who practice marching to a mission. In this session we will look at how we can begin to practice our mission and evaluate our growth.

First, how do we *put this skill to use*? Our trips overseas have been one of the best ways to grow in our mission-mindedness together. We saw poverty in Taipei and Moscow and were touched by the incredible need for the basics of life. Seeing the pain in the world helps keep our hearts tender toward people. It also enlarges our scope, pushing us beyond the concerns and ideas of our own backyards.

I (Matt) have also sought to get involved in activities beyond my comfort zone to hone my sense of mission and to learn through experience. For instance, I had been in the school band three years when I had to decide whether to remain in the program. I weighed the pros and cons of staying or leaving, and eventually decided to leave. I based my decision mainly on my realization that I would not grow much more as either a musician or leader in band. So I chose a variety of other activities my senior year which helped me solidify my mission statement.

But how do you keep *evaluating your progress* in this area? Remember the saying, "It is not what we expect, but what we inspect." We have to hold each other accountable in progressing toward goals.

Much of Ron's and Matt's growth and consistency in this area is due to continually redressing the area of mission. This is done through our scheduling, support systems, and replication activities.

First is *scheduling*. Ron has worked for years to let his schedule flow out of his mission. Often we try to prioritize our schedules, but this is wrong. We need to schedule our priorities. We must start with our mission as we have described it and then let weekly goals and activities flow out of the same. Then, we must prioritize these activities and build them into our schedules.

If you don't schedule it, you probably won't do it. So, if a date with a member of your family or a friend is important, schedule it.

A second accountability strategy is *support systems*. These include a daily time of prayer and reflection, keeping a journal, and having a small accountability group. We all need support systems. We try to support one another, but both of us have other people who help us move toward our mission. Ron, for instance, has two accountability groups: he meets weekly with two other men and has a conference call weekly with a different set of men. These meetings always begin with the question, "How are you doing on your specific goal?" The accountability, encouragement, and friendship Ron gets from these groups is invaluable.

Finally, *get involved helping others grow*. Matt served as a peer group counselor and met weekly with other school kids to help them get their lives in order and live with a sense of mission. Ron does the same thing through the studies he leads, books he writes, videos he produces, and speeches he gives. This ultimate accountability creates one of the best mechanisms for growth. As you share with others, you apply the truths, and the teaching reinforces the impact of these truths.

I (Matt) started a student prayer group on Sundays at home. By doing so, I began to fulfill both my purpose and vision statement. It forced me to know what I was doing because the people who came to the prayer group often looked to me for guidance. It also clarified my own purpose statement, and seeing people get something out of the prayer time was tangible and positive reinforcement.

Putting This to Work

1. Read Galatians 6:1–6. Why do we need one another and self-evaluation to grow?

2. What specific things did you do since the last session to march to a mission (read an article, talked with someone about it, wrote down several goals, built key goals into the schedule, etc.)? Make a list of everything you did.

☞ 3. What experiences could you both have together that would enhance your mission in life? For example, what about a day at a soup kitchen to develop a heart for people, a week in Washington, D.C., to build concern for politics, a missions trip to Estonia to grow in compassion for those in Eastern Europe, or hosting an exchange student or missionary? Brainstorm this area. Keep notes and talk about how you build these ideas into your schedule.

✎ 4. Look at the following "Weekly Goal Sheet." First, make a copy of the blank goal sheet and save it for use in chapter 7. Then follow the following procedures:

- List your roles (from session 2—*Family, Firm,* etc.) in the left-hand column.

- List the major life goals and then activities for each goal for the week.

- Prioritize the activities.

- Schedule the priorities, that is, write them into your schedule. Do not let the activities of the day (work, school, demands) push your other priorities from your schedule.

- Do this for one week and then evaluate your performance with a different color pen to record the actual way you spent your day.

✎ 5. Examine your support systems.

- Do you have a daily time alone to reflect, think, study? When? Where? What do you do? (If the answer here is no, make a commitment to have one now.)

- Do you keep a journal identifying how you are growing in your life and mission?

- Who are the other people to whom you are mutually accountable? What do you do? (If you don't have a group, list some potential people to be in such a group.)

☞ 6. What are you doing to help others grow? Could you start a study group, maybe a father-son study using this tool or some others? Brainstorm this for a while and take a specific step.

FINAL PROJECT: MARCH TO A MISSION

The goal: to give you such a vivid idea of what you want ultimately that you begin to move toward it consciously and unconsciously. This process will increase the mental and emotional desire to attain desireable qualities and will empower you to accomplish your mission.

Write down all the qualities that you want to be true of your life at the end (such as good family, close friends, great health, strong servant attitude, and so forth).

Every day, clip out a picture from a magazine, newspaper, advertisement, and so forth, that illustrates a quality that you have identified as important to you ultimately.

Create a scrapbook. Call it *My Vision*.

MAXIMIZERS Weekly Goal Sheet

Roles	Weekly Activities	Priority	Mon.	Tues.	Wed.	Thurs.	Fri.	Sat.	Sun.
Faith			6 A.M.	6 A.M.	6 A.M.	6 A.M.	6 A.M.	6 A.M.	6 A.M.
			7 A.M.	7 A.M.	7 A.M.	7 A.M.	7 A.M.	7 A.M.	7 A.M.
Fitness			8 A.M.	8 A.M.	8 A.M.	8 A.M.	8 A.M.	8 A.M.	8 A.M.
			9 A.M.	9 A.M.	9 A.M.	9 A.M.	9 A.M.	9 A.M.	9 A.M.
Family			10 A.M.	10 A.M.	10 A.M.	10 A.M.	10 A.M.	10 A.M.	10 A.M.
			11 A.M.	11 A.M.	11 A.M.	11 A.M.	11 A.M.	11 A.M.	11 A.M.
Friends			12 P.M.	12 P.M.	12 P.M.	12 P.M.	12 P.M.	12 P.M.	12 P.M.
			1 P.M.	1 P.M.	1 P.M.	1 P.M.	1 P.M.	1 P.M.	1 P.M.
Firm			2 P.M.	2 P.M.	2 P.M.	2 P.M.	2 P.M.	2 P.M.	2 P.M.
			3 P.M.	3 P.M.	3 P.M.	3 P.M.	3 P.M.	3 P.M.	3 P.M.
Finances			4 P.M.	4 P.M.	4 P.M.	4 P.M.	4 P.M.	4 P.M.	4 P.M.
			5 P.M.	5 P.M.	5 P.M.	5 P.M.	5 P.M.	5 P.M.	5 P.M.
Favor			6 P.M.	6 P.M.	6 P.M.	6 P.M.	6 P.M.	6 P.M.	6 P.M.
			7 P.M.	7 P.M.	7 P.M.	7 P.M.	7 P.M.	7 P.M.	7 P.M.

CHAPTER SEVEN

INTEGRATE ALL OF LIFE

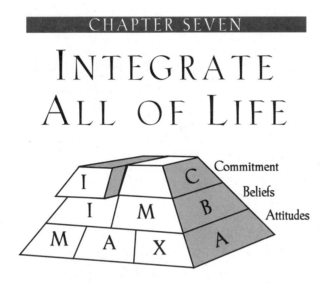

When I (Matt) was a junior in high school, I started dating a girl for the first time. It was a severe case of puppy love. I poured all my emotional energy into her. Then one day she ended the relationship. I was speechless. I felt emotionally destroyed. Even though she still wanted to "just be friends," I could hardly look at her, much less maintain a friendship with her. It took me about four months to be ready to pursue a friendship with her, but by that time she was angry and refused to speak to me. To be honest, in the midst of my willingness to start a friendship, I still thought about how upset I was at this girl for hurting me. The situation dominated my conversations, my thoughts—all of my life. So, for about seven months, I focused only on my relationship with this one girl and on feeling sorry for myself. I ignored virtually everything else and seriously missed out on all life had to offer.

Integrating all of life is really about having it all. Having it all involves living a full life and a balanced life. It is so easy to focus on just a couple of things in life and forget about everything else. Even if the things are good, a focus on them can be bad if you do not have a balanced life. That's why we address success in a broad range of areas, not just one or two. The next few chapters will address balancing life in three basic areas: your priorities, your attitudes, and your goals.

We think having balance in all areas of life is important, although most people think that specializing is important. Often people learn one particular employment really well, then ignore the other vital aspects of life, including their family and friends. It's very similar to the sports world. Most athletes specialize in one sport. For instance, many guys train their whole lives for one race, such as the hundred-yard dash. Instead we should be decathletes—the guys who have to be awesome in ten different events. The same holds true for our lives. If we are weak in any one life event, we won't be able to "win." Winning involves leading a balanced life.

If we don't lead a balanced life, however, we'll either get burned out or, even worse, live without a sense of passion for life. Remember the metaphor of the car battery from chapter 2? If our life is balanced, our personal car battery will continue to generate. If it isn't balanced, the battery runs down. It takes constant adjusting to keep the battery from running down. Balance is the practice of constantly adjusting.

This chapter will focus on the following areas:

- Balance Priorities—Personal and Professional

- Balance Attitudes—Structure and Spontaneity

- Balance Goals—Results and Relationships

Putting This to Work

1. The seven points on this circular chart are seven different roles in life. (*Faith, Family, Finances*, etc.)

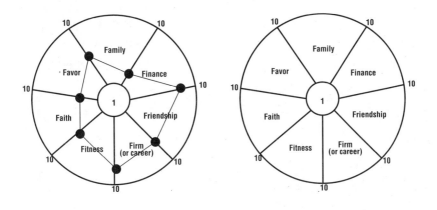

2. Using a red pen or pencil, draw dots on the spokes to rate your proficiency in that role. Start with the spoke to the left of the word *Family* to rate *Family*, then rate *Favor* on the spoke below the word *Favor*, and so on around the circle—rating your role on a scale of 1 to 10 (best). See completed example. Now, switch books with your father/son. Using a blue pen or pencil, mark a dot on each line where you perceive your father/son to be in that area. Finally, explain your assessment of yourself and of your father/son.

3. Trace this wheel (without your rating dots) six times on a blank piece of paper. Update your progress everyday this

week by marking a new balance wheel. Compare it to the one done before. Share your progress and encourage growth in balancing and integrating your lives.

SESSION 1: BALANCE PRIORITIES— PERSONAL AND PROFESSIONAL

If you stood on your right leg, lifted your left leg, kept your left arm at your side, and raised your right arm straight out—and then someone put books on your outstretched right hand, one by one, balancing would be difficult, wouldn't it?

One of the most obvious areas where you need a sense of balance is in your priorities. But to do this, you need to take some very definite steps. First, you must *rule your impulses*. You will need a disciplined outlook on life and a sense of urgency about accomplishing your goals, but you also should not be so driven that you lose control of your perspective and priorities.

For instance, if you are like us, you tend to push yourself to get things done. Sometimes work or school can so consume us that we lose focus on our personal growth and development. The other day Ron realized that he was making some very poor decisions because he hadn't given attention to his physical, emotional, and spiritual health. The result was a lack of perspective and numerous poor choices. Be careful here. Your effectiveness will be in significant proportion to your ability to self-manage or discipline all vital areas of your life.

Second, you must reorder your priorities. It makes things a lot easier if you think of your priorities as three concentric circles, instead of thinking of them as items on a numbered list. The outside circle represents the other people in your life, the middle circle is you, and the center circle represents God, or the spiritual core of your life.

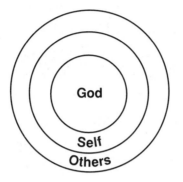

The center of your life should be God. Jesus said, "Love the Lord your God with all your heart and with all your soul and with all your mind and with all your strength" (Mark 12:30). Now, you may think, *I don't even believe in God.* Sure you do! Look at it this way: whatever is at the center of your life is your god. So, what is at the core of your life? Is it work, school, family, church, money, an intimate relationship with a supernatural being, or what?

It is critical to decide what is at the core of your life. By the way, if you can't determine what or who is your god, then you must be your god. And that should make you nervous. Don't get us wrong. You are probably a terrific person. But we sure wouldn't want you or any other living person to be our god. Nor do we recommend that we be your god. We aren't that good, great, wise, or powerful.

We've discovered the need for a personal relationship with God in our own lives, and have formed that relationship by inviting Jesus Christ to be our Saviour. As we have put our faith in the fact that He died on the cross to save us from our sins, we have experienced a whole new level of living. We aren't perfect (far from it), but we know we are loved, forgiven, and empowered to be the kind of men we know we should be.

When we love God, we experience that power. When we don't, we don't experience it.

Whoever or whatever is your god needs to be your center. So choose well. And once you've chosen the boss of your life, then submit to that boss. That means put God in the center.

You also need to love yourself, which does not mean that you should tell the world how wonderful you think you are. Truly loving yourself is caring for yourself. After all, if you're not loving and caring for yourself, you can't grow and keep yourself sharp. If you can't keep yourself sharp, you certainly can't help others, and you can't maintain balance in your priorities.

The outside circle is for your love of others, referring to everyone else: people you see every day, people you like or dislike, your parents, your children, and so forth.

If you want to reorder your priorities everyday, you need to love God, yourself, and others.

Once again, *readjust your schedule to fit your priorities*. Don't readjust your priorities to fit your schedule. At the beginning of each week, use your vision, purpose, life roles, and life goals to determine a list of activities for the week. To determine these activities, you must ask yourself two questions:

- What is the greatest need right now?
- Where is there previous neglect? What have I let go?

Once you determine these activities, *follow through!* Do them! You *will* begin to balance your priorities and your life when you follow through.

Putting This to Work

1. Read Matthew 6:19–24. What is the threefold priority system here? Do you follow it?

2. Identify your most important goal in the areas of personal, family, and work/school.

_____

_____

_____

_____

3. With the "Weekly Goal Sheet" we've provided (or your own), write your goals into your schedule

4. Commit to talk daily about whether you're accomplishing these goals.

SESSION 2:
BALANCE ATTITUDES—
STRUCTURE AND SPONTANEITY

Structure and spontaneity are the tensions that face our attitudes.

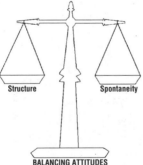

Structure   Spontaneity

BALANCING ATTITUDES

Have you ever planned to get something done during a day, built it into your schedule, and then not accomplished it? Of course that's happened to you—unless you aren't breathing.

In fact, that is a typical occurrence for most of us. Ron recalls planning out a day recently when everything he planned didn't

MAXIMIZERS Weekly Goal Sheet

Roles	Weekly Activities	Priority	Mon.	Tues.	Wed.	Thurs.	Fri.	Sat.	Sun.
Faith			6 A.M.	6 A.M.	6 A.M.	6 A.M.	6 A.M.	6 A.M.	6 A.M.
			7 A.M.	7 A.M.	7 A.M.	7 A.M.	7 A.M.	7 A.M.	7 A.M.
Fitness			8 A.M.	8 A.M.	8 A.M.	8 A.M.	8 A.M.	8 A.M.	8 A.M.
			9 A.M.	9 A.M.	9 A.M.	9 A.M.	9 A.M.	9 A.M.	9 A.M.
Family			10 A.M.	10 A.M.	10 A.M.	10 A.M.	10 A.M.	10 A.M.	10 A.M.
			11 A.M.	11 A.M.	11 A.M.	11 A.M.	11 A.M.	11 A.M.	11 A.M.
Friends			12 P.M.	12 P.M.	12 P.M.	12 P.M.	12 P.M.	12 P.M.	12 P.M.
			1 P.M.	1 P.M.	1 P.M.	1 P.M.	1 P.M.	1 P.M.	1 P.M.
Firm			2 P.M.	2 P.M.	2 P.M.	2 P.M.	2 P.M.	2 P.M.	2 P.M.
			3 P.M.	3 P.M.	3 P.M.	3 P.M.	3 P.M.	3 P.M.	3 P.M.
Finances			4 P.M.	4 P.M.	4 P.M.	4 P.M.	4 P.M.	4 P.M.	4 P.M.
			5 P.M.	5 P.M.	5 P.M.	5 P.M.	5 P.M.	5 P.M.	5 P.M.
Favor			6 P.M.	6 P.M.	6 P.M.	6 P.M.	6 P.M.	6 P.M.	6 P.M.
			7 P.M.	7 P.M.	7 P.M.	7 P.M.	7 P.M.	7 P.M.	7 P.M.

occur because of so many interruptions. But were they really interruptions? When a friend called with a need for someone to listen, was that an interruption? When he felt sick and needed to rest, was that an interruption? When he was puzzled, unmotivated, frustrated, and needed to stop and search out some wisdom in the Bible and pray, was that an interruption?

No, these weren't interruptions. They were opportunities to do what he really needed to do. This brings us to the issue of balancing the attitudes we have toward life, specifically concerning structure and spontaneity.

We tend to be either very structured or very spontaneous. Those of us who are structured strive to finish a to-do list everyday, remain busy at all hours, and become superior time managers. Those of us who are spontaneous lack any form in our lives. We do whatever pleases us at the moment and put off anything that doesn't seem fun. Either method is faulty: if you're so structured that you can't stop to spend time with someone who needs you or if you're so spontaneous that you can't accomplish things with a deadline, you're not balanced. Balanced people manage a happy medium between these two extremes.

To get a healthy balance, incorporate the following three actions in your life: tighten goals and loosen plans, think process not just product, and treat interruptions as guests (respond not react).

We really love the idea *of tightening goals and loosening plans* because it frees up a lot of life. For instance, in the opening scenario of this session, Ron talked about all the interruptions he had one day—sickness, confusion, phone calls, and so forth, that threw his schedule out of whack. We believe that having a schedule is important and that aiming at goals is critical to our progression. We need to write out our goals, prioritize them, and build them into our schedule. But we need to stay loose with our plans. For example, during that day, Ron had clear, tight goals, but he knew he needed to buy up the opportunities around him. He let his plans flex to accomplish what was really important.

Most of life does not happen as scheduled: it happens in those moments around the dinner table, on the way to work or school, in the midst of struggles and joys. You can keep the structure there by tightening your goals and clearly defining those things you must do to succeed, while loosening your plans to leave room for spontaneity. This gives you room and direction for the constant midcourse adjustments in life.

Next, you need to learn to *think process, not product*. There's an old saying that the end justifies the means, meaning you can do whatever you want if it accomplishes what you want. That is trash! What you really need is a successful, healthy process (by making the right choices in your daily life) for a successful product. As we've mentioned before, focus on the roots of your life, not the fruit. If you focus on the roots, the fruit will ripen in due time. Live every minute of your life—whether alone or in a crowd—in accordance with the kind of person you want to be.

Finally, balancing attitudes has a lot to do with learning *to treat interruptions as guests*. We often think that any kind of interruption hinders us and keeps us from accomplishing something. Maybe you play tennis. If you play right-handed and break your right arm, you'd be pretty upset. But what if you treated this "interruption" as a guest. You could learn to play tennis left-handed and add a weapon to your tennis arsenal! To see interruptions as guests, you change your perspective. Sometimes interruptions are just invitations to stop and smell the roses. Don't be afraid to. All three of these attitude adjusters are really simple perspective shifts that can make a world of difference in your life.

Putting This to Work

1. Read Ephesians 5:15–17. How can you live wisely?

2. Make a list of the interruptions you experienced this week. How did you respond? Why did you respond that way? Was the interruption a negative or positive one?

_____

_____

_____

_____

_____

_____

_____

3. Put an "x" where you would fall on this line of structure vs. spontaneity. Put a circle where your father/son would fall on the line as well. Then discuss your assessments.

Structure   **Spontaneity**

◁————————————————————————————▷

4. Identify three unique opportunities you had this last week to spontaneously meet the need of someone. Did you do it? If so, are you glad you did? If not, why not? Do you wish you had? Write down and share your answers.

1. _____

_____

_____

_____

2. _____

_____

_____

_____

3. _____

_____

_____

_____

☞   5. What one thing can you do this week to be more sponta-
    neous if you are structured or to be more structured if you
    are spontaneous? Share this with each other.

SESSION 3:
BALANCE GOALS—RESULTS AND RELATIONSHIPS

Most of us have little problem with *result goals*. We say, "I want
to lose twenty pounds" or "I want to get all A's and B's this semester." *Relational goals*, however, are something in which we definitely
do not excel. You may say, "I want to be nicer this year," but have
you made specific goals showing how you want to invest your time
and energy with people? The vast majority of unbalanced people in

America are that way not because they have a lack of result goals, but because they fail at relational goals.

Result goals have to be balanced with relational goals.

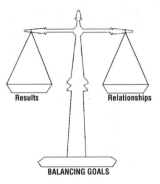

Results Relationships

BALANCING GOALS

Three steps to help fathers and sons become balanced in their goals include listing your goals (result and relationship) in your schedule, listening to your left and right brain, and loving people and using things.

First, *listing your goals in your schedule* will balance your goals and, subsequently, your schedule. Identify your priorities and goals and find concrete ways to insert them into your schedule. Be especially careful to set aside specific times to spend with different people. Don't kid yourself: if you don't mark it in, you won't do it.

Second, *listen to your left and right brain.* The left brain will be the more logical side—the structured side of your attitude. The right brain is the more intuitive side, the creative side that thinks more conceptually. To have balanced attitudes, you must allow yourself to be creative and structured, to dream and to be realistic. A combination of these two extremes gives you balance. You benefit from the best of both realms. Being too focused on one or the other, however, forces you to reap the cons more than the pros of the singular mode of thinking.

Finally, learn to *love people and use things*. This sounds strange at first, but what we want to help you do is learn to love people and use things, instead of loving things and using people. Remember, things come and go, but our relationships and the effect we have on people last. When people look back on their lives, they are always impacted by the same things: family, friends, relationships, quality, and character. These are life's rewards. These are the things that count. How much is your life counting?

Putting This to Work

1. Read Romans 12:9–21. What are the key qualities in a loving relationship?

2. Name the five most important people in your life. Be sure to include at least one person from outside the home. You may write down more than five names if you wish.

   1. _____

      _____

   2. _____

      _____

   3. _____

      _____

   4. _____

      _____

   5. _____

      _____

✎ 3. If you could change anything about the relationships in your family, what would you change? How and why?

_____

_____

_____

✎ 4. Now, identify one specific, measurable goal for each change you would like to make to improve your family relationships.

_____

_____

☞ 5. Share your answers. Commit to do these things this week. Get together with your father/son each day to report on how you're doing.

FINAL PROJECT: INTEGRATE ALL OF LIFE— SCHEDULING YOUR PRIORITIES

For one week, using the MAXIMIZERS Weekly Goal Sheet, write down nightly on the goal sheet what you did during the day. Don't write down what you wanted to do, but what you actually did. Then the next week, write down two or three goals for personal, family, and work/school improvements. Prioritize that list with "1" for the most important, "2" for the second most important, and so on. Write each of these into your schedule.

At the end of each day, write down what you actually did in red over the schedule. Do this the next week too. Don't forget to share with each other nightly.

MAXIMIZERS Weekly Goal Sheet

Roles	Weekly Activities	Priority	Mon.	Tues.	Wed.	Thurs.	Fri.	Sat.	Sun.
Faith			6 A.M.	6 A.M.	6 A.M.	6 A.M.	6 A.M.	6 A.M.	6 A.M.
			7 A.M.	7 A.M.	7 A.M.	7 A.M.	7 A.M.	7 A.M.	7 A.M.
Fitness			8 A.M.	8 A.M.	8 A.M.	8 A.M.	8 A.M.	8 A.M.	8 A.M.
			9 A.M.	9 A.M.	9 A.M.	9 A.M.	9 A.M.	9 A.M.	9 A.M.
Family			10 A.M.	10 A.M.	10 A.M.	10 A.M.	10 A.M.	10 A.M.	10 A.M.
			11 A.M.	11 A.M.	11 A.M.	11 A.M.	11 A.M.	11 A.M.	11 A.M.
Friends			12 P.M.	12 P.M.	12 P.M.	12 P.M.	12 P.M.	12 P.M.	12 P.M.
			1 P.M.	1 P.M.	1 P.M.	1 P.M.	1 P.M.	1 P.M.	1 P.M..
Firm			2 P.M.	2 P.M.	2 P.M.	2 P.M.	2 P.M.	2 P.M.	2 P.M.
			3 P.M.	3 P.M.	3 P.M.	3 P.M.	3 P.M.	3 P.M.	3 P.M.
Finances			4 P.M.	4 P.M.	4 P.M.	4 P.M.	4 P.M.	4 P.M.	4 P.M.
			5 P.M.	5 P.M.	5 P.M.	5 P.M.	5 P.M.	5 P.M.	5 P.M.
Favor			6 P.M.	6 P.M.	6 P.M.	6 P.M.	6 P.M.	6 P.M.	6 P.M.
			7 P.M.	7 P.M.	7 P.M.	7 P.M.	7 P.M.	7 P.M.	7 P.M.

MAXIMIZERS Weekly Goal Sheet

Roles	Weekly Activities	Priority	Mon.	Tues.	Wed.	Thurs.	Fri.	Sat.	Sun.
Faith			6 A.M.	6 A.M.	6 A.M.	6 A.M.	6 A.M.	6 A.M.	6 A.M.
			7 A.M.	7 A.M.	7 A.M.	7 A.M.	7 A.M.	7 A.M.	7 A.M.
Fitness			8 A.M.	8 A.M.	8 A.M.	8 A.M.	8 A.M.	8 A.M.	8 A.M.
			9 A.M.	9 A.M.	9 A.M.	9 A.M.	9 A.M.	9 A.M.	9 A.M.
Family			10 A.M.	10 A.M.	10 A.M.	10 A.M.	10 A.M.	10 A.M.	10 A.M.
			11 A.M.	11 A.M.	11 A.M.	11 A.M.	11 A.M.	11 A.M.	11 A.M.
Friends			12 P.M.	12 P.M.	12 P.M.	12 P.M.	12 P.M.	12 P.M.	12 P.M.
			1 P.M.	1 P.M.	1 P.M.	1 P.M.	1 P.M.	1 P.M.	1 P.M..
Firm			2 P.M.	2 P.M.	2 P.M.	2 P.M.	2 P.M.	2 P.M.	2 P.M.
			3 P.M.	3 P.M.	3 P.M.	3 P.M.	3 P.M.	3 P.M.	3 P.M.
Finances			4 P.M.	4 P.M.	4 P.M.	4 P.M.	4 P.M.	4 P.M.	4 P.M.
			5 P.M.	5 P.M.	5 P.M.	5 P.M.	5 P.M.	5 P.M.	5 P.M.
Favor			6 P.M.	6 P.M.	6 P.M.	6 P.M.	6 P.M.	6 P.M.	6 P.M.
			7 P.M.	7 P.M.	7 P.M.	7 P.M.	7 P.M.	7 P.M.	7 P.M.

CHAPTER EIGHT

ZERO IN ON CARING FOR PEOPLE

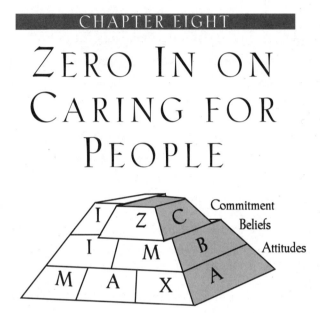

Do you have anyone in your life who drives you nuts? Is there a relationship in your home or at work or school that you would like to improve? Do you feel that your present family life reflects the qualities of a real team?

What all these questions have in common is the area of relationships. Let's face it: guys don't put much effort and energy into relationships. If you do, you are the exception. Most men claim that relationships, especially with friends and families, are extremely important to us, yet few of us actually invest the time to make these relationships work.

We are convinced that people who maximize their lives have the principle of caring for people built into the foundation of their existence. People who are maximizers make a point of loving others and putting others first. Maximizers realize they need people for support and encouragement, and people need them too. This sense of common need provides a healthy unity among people.

Basically, unity is a concern more for people as a whole than for self. People who are concerned about unity see others as individuals with needs and talents, instead of as just another person or number. They know that each person has as much right to be genuinely cared for as they do.

Unity, however, is not uniformity. Uniformity means that we all do things the same way. But you don't have to do things exactly like your father/son; your differences make you unique. Uniformity takes away the individual gifts and talents that each person brings to a relationship.

Also, unity is not unanimity. Unanimity means that we always agree, and by saying that we need to agree on everything, we imply that certain opinions aren't good or valid. In unity, on the other hand, we are committed to help each other live a complete, maximized life.

This chapter will focus on the commitment principle of zeroing in on caring for people. We will use this acrostic as a basis for practicing U.N.I.T.Y. in the next few sessions:

Uplift each other

Need each other

Intimately relate to each other

Trust each other

Yield to each other

Putting This to Work

1. Read 1 John 2:9–11. How important is caring for other people?

2. Think about a team (athletic, business, church, etc.) that you were part of in the past. What was it like? Now brainstorm the qualities of a great team. What are the team members like? How do they work together?

_____

_____

_____

_____

_____

3. Choose three relationships (one at home, one at work/school, one in the social arena) that you would like to change. List the people involved and what you'd change about the relationship. Discuss your insights with your dad/son.

1. _____

_____

2. _____

_____

3. _____

_____

☞ 4. On a scale of one to ten, how would you define the harmony in your relationship with your father/son, ranging from 1 (poor harmony) to 10 (great harmony).

Poor ←— **1 2 3 4 5 6 7 8 9 10** —→ **Great**

- Why did you rate your relationship like that? Discuss this for a few minutes.

✎ 5. What one action will you take this week to make your relationship even more harmonious (for example, making a point of understanding the other's point of view, listening more than speaking, etc.)? Identify the action and specify how and when you plan to do this. Be committed to make it happen. Keep a record here of your progress.

Day	Action	Progress
1	_____	_____
2	_____	_____
3	_____	_____
4	_____	_____
5	_____	_____
6	_____	_____
7	_____	_____

Session 1: Uplift Each Other— Complimenting and Expressing Confidence

Do you know how fleas are trained? They are put into a jar with a lid sealed on it. Then the little critters jump up and down in the jar, hitting their heads on the lid. Eventually, one of the brighter fleas says, "Wait a second. If we jump a little lower, we will get our aerobic exercise and won't hurt our heads." So they jump lower.

After a while, the fleas' trainers remove the lid. At that moment, those minuscule acrobats could jump right out of that jar and go find a mangy ole' hound to feast on. But they don't. Why? Because they have been trained to jump lower, not higher.

That is exactly what happens to many of us. As kids we have big dreams and hopes, but as life goes on, we're exposed to people who tell us we're not that hot or we're too fat, too small, too poor, too messed up, or just plain hopeless . . . and we start to believe it. We figuratively jump lower.

When other people encourage us, they combat the ugly, debilitating messages in our heads. They uplift us by complimenting, comforting, coaching, and expressing confidence in us.

Son and Dad, you both need to become real pros at uplifting each other!

Two Greek words, *para kaleo*, express the concept of uplifting each other. *Para* is Greek for *alongside*, and *kaleo* means *to call*. *Para kaleo* occurs when someone comes alongside another to encourage and support him. There are four components of uplifting one another: complimenting, expressing confidence, comforting, and coaching.

Complimenting, an underestimated and misunderstood art, is the key to uplifting others. Effective complimenting isn't building people up because of their looks or talents; it's commending people for their character—for who they are on the inside.

Examine your attitude when you talk to people. Do you tend to cut people down or build them up? (Do you sometimes use sarcasm as a primary source of humor?) Please realize that both positive and negative comments influence how people view themselves. Are you complimenting or cutting with your language?

The American Institute of Family Relations asked parents how many positive versus negative statements they made to their children. The research results are familiar: the average parent made ten negative statements to every one positive statement.

Elementary teachers in another setting were asked how many positive statements it takes to overcome a negative statement. That research indicated it takes four positive statements to counteract every negative statement.[1]

Chew on this resulting ratio: children hear ten negative statements for every positive remark, yet it takes four positive statements to overcome one negative. Conclusion: we can't ignore the impact of our words. To impact people for good, compliment them. Here's how:

- Be positive (focus on some area of character, like faithfulness or hard work or friendship).

- Be practical. Say something like, "Dad, I appreciate the way you spend so much time with me." Or, "Son, thanks for being so consistent in loving your sister and honoring your mom."

- Be persistent. Every day seek to compliment those people around you. That's right! Every day. Use some variety: say it, write it, sing it. Be creative.

The second way to build people up is by *expressing confidence* in them. How do you respond when your father/son makes a mistake? Often, we tend to express frustration, disappointment, and anger when the other makes mistakes, but that expression doesn't build unity. As long as someone is genuinely sorry for his mistake, it's vital to express the confidence that says you believe in him.

Earvin "Magic" Johnson is considered by many to be the best basketball player ever to play the game. People constantly point to his ability to raise the level of performance among his teammates. Why? Because Magic played the game with immeasurable faith in his teammates, and he expressed this verbally time and time again, even when his teammates messed up. He knew that one of the ways to build unity is by expressing confidence in people.

One of the most fascinating Bible stories is that of Jesus' visit to his disciples after his resurrection. It grabs me because of the way he responded to that group after they had deserted him. Imagine that you were Jesus facing your faithless disciples. You knew very well how most of these men you loved had treated you. You'd poured your life into them. You'd put all your eggs in the basket of these disciples, and they, who watched your miracles and trusted you to tell the truth, not only didn't believe you would be raised from the dead, but actually turned on you. Now you're back to see them before you go to heaven. How would you have responded to them? If I were in his position, I would have been tempted to say something like this: "Yeah, it's Jesus and I'm here for one reason: to tell you that you're all out. You're out of the game. You're off the team. You're through with the program. Good-bye. I poured my life into you guys. I fed the five thousand, healed the sick, brought dead people to life, told you I'd die, told you I'd come back . . . and what was your response? You people are pathetic.

"OK, Thomas, once and for all, why don't you come up here and feel my hands. Thomas, you're a negative guy. You're an administrator, that's what you are. You've been griping and complaining since we started. You always see the problems.

"Peter, what are you laughing about over there? Good night! You're impetuous, you're a loud mouth, you denied me three times in front of a little girl, and you're a coward. You're fired, Peter.

"And you're out, Thomas.

"In fact, you're all out!"

That's what I would have wanted to say.

What did Jesus do? He looked at them and said, "All authority in heaven and earth is given to me and I give it to you. Go and make disciples of all nations." In essence, he told them that the history of mankind was in their hands and that he had enough faith in them to pass the spiritual baton to all humanity.

How do you handle it when people fail you? Jesus believed in people and consequently developed a movement that has changed the course of history.

Try complimenting, comforting, coaching, and expressing confidence in your dad/son and others, and see the changes your uplifting statements bring.

Putting This to Work

1. Read Hebrews 3:13 and 1 Thessalonians 5:13–15. Why should you compliment others? How and when should you do it?

2. When was the last time someone said something encouraging to you? How did it make you feel?

_____

_____

3. When was the last time you built up your dad/son with words of encouragement? How did he respond? When was the last time you said something sarcastic, demeaning, or critical? How did your dad/son respond to those remarks?

_____

_____

_____

4. Where do you need to have your confidence built up? How can your dad/son help with this? Try to think of specific things that could be said or done, then discuss them with your dad/son.

SESSION 2:
COMFORTING AND COACHING

Have you ever felt down? Sure you have. What do you want and need when you are blue? If you are like us, you need understanding and support. You don't need advice.

We men have a strong tendency to want to fix things, so when someone else is down, we try to fix him. Big mistake.

More often than not, we need to be there for the other person when he is down. We need to listen, empathize, and love him.

We like the definition of friendship that says, "A true friend is someone who knows all about me, loves me for who I am, and has no plans for my immediate improvement." Isn't that what you really want?

The third way to uplift people is by *comforting* them. Sooner or later, we all go through troubles and need a friend to support us. Much of comforting is simply listening to people and letting them vent their problems.

The first couple of days that Matt spent at UCLA he was absolutely miserable. He felt hopeless, alone, and altogether depressed. Ron was in town to visit for a couple of days, and before he left, he and Matt sat down to pray. Ron asked God to *comfort* Matt. Matt then started to cry (this is an OK thing to do, guys!) because it comforted him that Ron cared enough to pray for him. Ron's prayer uplifted Matt.

The final method of uplifting others is by *coaching* them. Coaching others happens when you determine what is needed and help people get there in the best way possible. In fact, fathers and sons coach each other in many ways—through a son's learning to drive a car or a dad's learning to relax.

To effectively coach a person you must first determine what is needed and articulate a goal for improving the situation. Then use the appropriate means to achieve this goal. The good part is that you become centered on whomever you're trying to coach instead of being focused on yourself. You are helping the other person achieve this goal at his pace.

Now, think about a good coach you know. What does he do? He may use what we call the I.D.E.A. approach to developing people (as was discussed in the book's introduction). He *i*nstructs you on what to do. He *d*emonstrates how to do it. He helps you *e*xperience it, and then he *a*ssesses (evaluates) how you are doing. He keeps doing this with you until you become skilled in each area of the game.

The IDEA method is effective in coaching others in any skill.

Putting This to Work

✎ 1. When was the last time you were really hurt and needed comfort? What happened? Did anyone help? Did you express your hurt or bury it?

_____

_____

_____

_____

_____

_____

☞ 2. What could your father/son have done to comfort you (spent time together, listened, given you space, etc.)? Share these insights.

☞ 3. What are the characteristics of a great coach? Brainstorm these together.

✎ 4. List one area where you could use some help or coaching. Do you need information, encouragement, or an example? Share this together, and tell each other how you will help coach the other in this area.

_____

_____

_____

_____

Session 3:
Need Each Other

In England's Warwick Castle a series of steep steps leads down to a dank dungeon. A narrow crevasse opening onto a small floor space is cut into the wall in the far corner of the dungeon. Rusted iron grating covers a hole in the floor. An adult man would have just enough room to crouch or maybe sit there. This hole is a French torture device called the *oubliette*, a noun form of the French verb, *oublier*, meaning "to forget." The process of torture in the oubliette is simple. No physical pain is involved. The prisoner need fear no broken bones. He need not agonize as he waits for his fate to be revealed to him. The prisoner is merely placed in the small hole in the corner of the dungeon. Then he is forgotten.

Too often, fathers and sons forget each other. Don't be fooled by the idea that you are only hurting each other when you argue—forgetting about each other is just as damaging. When you forget your father/son, you deny your need for interaction with him. To promote healthy relations between fathers and sons, a recognition of *the need* for each other is necessary. Needing each other happens when you build a strong, healthy interdependence with other people in your life. More broadly, needing each other means knowing that other people need you and that you need other people. Yes, it's a basic concept, but we guys don't seem to understand it or the benefits we can reap from living this truth.

Other people do need you! Think about your daily activities. Normally, one-third of everything you do involves help from another person or persons. People need people to get things done. Your family and friends depend on you for emotional support and encouragement every day. However, we often find it too easy to shirk our responsibility and ignore the needs of others. We all have a responsibility to zero in on caring for people. People need us for this.

Others need you, but *you also need others!* Men often live as if they are Lone Rangers. It doesn't matter if you're ten or seventy, you will likely think that you can get through much of life all by yourself. You may act as if you don't need other people. Men tend to identify with Paul Simon, who proclaimed, "I am a rock. I am an island." But he was wrong.

You need people! It doesn't even make sense to try to live life on your own. Working with other people is almost always more productive, and working alone can often frustrate everyone. None of us has the strength to live without needing others. Nothing is worse than being totally on our own. So it is ridiculous for us to try to operate alone. We need people!

Cultivate meaningful friendships with your classmates, neighbors, business associates, family, and so forth. You have to make your friendships a priority. You can start doing this by practicing this UNITY acrostic we've been talking about. One great way to build strong, intimate friendships with those closest to you is to develop a system of accountability with them. Although we have already talked about accountability at length, it is important enough to reiterate here.

You should start a small accountability group right now with your dad/son. You need someone to help keep you in line. Tell each other where you really struggle in your life and have each other ask specific questions consistently about your improvement or lack thereof. For instance, if you have a real problem with cussing, Dad, try getting your son to ask you when you last cussed. Accountability puts you on the spot, but it also produces the interdependence your relationship needs to grow. Interdependence will bring fathers and sons closer than anything else in this book. That's what has happened to us.

Putting This to Work

1. Write down three specific ways you need one another.

   1. _____

   _____

   2. _____

   _____

   3. _____

   _____

2. Share your answers with each other. How can you help your father/son?

3. Write down one area in which your dad/son can support you and hold you accountable this week.

   _____

   _____

   _____

   _____

SESSION 4:
INTIMATELY RELATE TO OTHERS BY CONNECTING

When you look at this glass of water, what do you see? Is it half-empty or half-full? Both are true—it depends on your perspective. The trick is explaining your perspective to another person. It's even trickier to explain your perspective about the intimate struggles and joys of your life to another.

Talking about inner triumphs and troubles is another area in which all men—fathers and sons—tend to struggle. Intimately relating to each other is the bedrock of unity, but it's something we hardly ever practice because intimately relating involves putting your emotions, confidence, and ego on the line. Men frequently think, *If I don't relate to others on an intimate level, then I won't ever get hurt and people won't find out how messed up I really am.* Unfortunately, as easy and uncluttered as that idea may seem, it is actually a cowardly escape from (and blatant denial of) life and others. The only way you can really live life is by relating intimately with others—giving yourself wholeheartedly to them and allowing them to give themselves wholeheartedly to you. You can start to do this by mastering the art of communication. In communication, we develop and maintain intimate relations with certain people by connecting and clarifying.

Connecting involves two things—understanding and being understood. The order of these is vital. First you try to understand what *others* are attempting to communicate before you worry about being understood yourself. Connecting is all about seeing a situation from the perspective of the other person. It's stepping into his shoes and connecting with his point of view.

Connecting is a hard thing to do because we often think that the other person misunderstands what we're trying to communicate. We are so busy trying to be understood that we refuse to work on understanding. Sons, when your dad comes home from work dead tired after a long day, you may want to talk to him about some issue you are facing. To intimately relate to your dad, however, you need to look at the situation from his point of view. He's tired and has had a long day. He wants to put his feet up, relax, and watch the news. Jumping into someone else's shoes like this helps us appreciate the other person and be others-focused.

Fathers, if your son comes home from school foaming at the mouth in anger because the school bully picked on him again, just listen to him. He doesn't want to hear that it's no big deal or that you are going to call the teacher and have the bully punished. He wants you to let him vent his frustrations. Your son wants to be able to spout off and get out all his anger and hurt. Let him do it. Seek to understand your son's dilemma; don't worry about solving it. Listen to him, empathize with him, comfort him, and let him know you're there for him. This will build intimacy between you.

After you've achieved an understanding of the other person's point of view, *seek to be understood*. We think that people will understand exactly what we mean just by listening to what we say, when, in reality, our words themselves have very little to do with communication. We communicate much more strongly through our body language and other nonverbal methods.

Consider this: if one of you asks the other how he's doing, he might respond, "I'm great!" But this "I'm great!" could mean many different things. If said sincerely, it could mean that he really is doing well. If said sarcastically, it could mean that he's upset and angry. It's easy to miscommunicate with your tone of voice or body posture, so you need to make sure you are communicating what you want to communicate. Then you will be connecting with the other person.

Putting This to Work

☞ 1. When you look at this picture, what do you see? You may see an old lady's face or a beautiful young woman. Can you see both? Remember, what you see depends on your perspective.

☞ 2. What else do you view differently from your son/dad? Maybe it's music, TV shows, friends, or something else. Talk about your views. Focus on why you see things differently.

✎ 3. Do you feel that you understand your father/son and his perspective? Why or why not?

_____

_____

_____

✎   4. Do you feel that your father/son understands you and your
        perspective on issues? Why or why not?

_____

_____

_____

_____

_____

📖 5. Read Philippians 2:4.

SESSION 5:
INTIMATELY RELATE TO OTHERS BY CLARIFYING

When Matt was younger, he would frequently drive Ron nuts.
Matt had a bad temper and was pretty emotional. Ron, on the other
hand, tended to be more even-tempered. Actually, we were very different in many areas of personality. We grated on each other and
sometimes that resulted in conflict. It still can.

There have been times when we have poorly confronted one
another by losing our temper, yelling, and overreacting. That
doesn't help us grow together at all. Nor will it help you if you do
the same.

So let's discuss how we should resolve conflict.

In working through the previous chapters, you have built up your
communication level by connecting and you are beginning to intimately relate to each other. To keep this high level of communication going—to be really connecting continuously—you've got to be
clarifying. Clarifying is the best way to resolve the conflicts fathers
and sons might have. Clarifying is a combination of loving and
truthful communication.

Here is an example. Ron has a weight problem (as a child, his nickname was "Jelly Belly Jenson"), which Matt occasionally needles him about. Matt will playfully call Ron "huge" or "big guy." He doesn't mean any harm, but it is hurtful to Ron's self-esteem. One time Ron approached Matt and, in a loving yet direct manner, asked him to stop using words that poked fun at his weight. Ron kept his comments kind, clear, and direct. That is clarifying. Such caring, direct honesty will enable fathers and sons to intimately relate to each other.

Here are some practical steps for clarifying issues and resolving conflicts:

- Always practice clarification in private. Don't embarrass each other in public.

- Always be practical and constructive. Saying "You're a jerk!" isn't going to solve the problem or help clarify it.

- Be thoroughly honest, but be kind. Remember, we are all fragile. Harsh words and/or attitudes (watch the nonverbals) *never* build unity.

- Focus on one conflict area at a time.

- Don't run away from issues or beat up the other person (in any sense of the term). You are on the same team.

Here's an example that may help you out. "Son, I am so proud of the way you are growing into a man. There are so many qualities in your life I wish I had in mine, like your tenacity, commitment, and ability to make friends. There is one thing in your life, though, that I think you may not be aware of, and that I want to point out. In light of all of your great qualities this is small, but I want to urge you to think about and deal with this issue. It is how you treat your mother. I sense your anger and frustration at times, and I think she does also. I've heard you say things recently that have hurt your mom. For instance, when you argued with her two days ago, you made your case in such a way that she felt unloved and stupid. Now, you have every right to reason with us both. But, for your mother's sake and your own, I want you to work through this. And I'll help you. In fact, let me suggest that you think through how you want to speak to your mom in an honorable way and then practice it. In fact, why don't we do it right now. Then let me be your dad and your friend, and help you by holding you accountable to build a new habit here. What do you say?"

The bottom line is that you need to help each other grow. Sons, during your teen years you need to deal maturely with your dad and be an increasingly supportive, clarifying friend to him. And, dads, you need to let your son grow into manhood and increasingly treat him as an adult and friend, not as a child.

Clarifying and conflict resolution skills need to be adjusted in line with what we have just explained as your son grows into manhood. The same respect and attitude is needed with your son at any age.

Putting This to Work

1. Write down the last time you had a fight with one another. How did you feel? What do you think you did wrong? What do you think your dad/son did wrong? How could you both have improved?

_____

_____

_____

_____

2. Using the conflict you mentioned above, how would you handle it differently using the five clarifying steps?

_____

_____

_____

_____

_____

3. Share your insights with one another in a role-play situation. Practice what you would say and how you would say it. Evaluate each other. Keep it up until you build a good approach. Then use it the next time you need to clarify.

SESSION 6:
TRUST EACH OTHER

As Ron said in his book *Make a Life, Not Just a Living,* "The hinges on the door to intimate, unified relationships are greased by the level of trust that you have in and with those around you."

If you want to zero in on caring for people and build unity between yourselves, you have to trust one another on a very high level. (Of course, you have to earn and deserve that trust.)

Trust isn't just about believing what a person says; it's about believing the best about each other. Have you ever made a huge assumption about someone you've never spoken to? Often, when you are finally introduced to him, all of your imaginings turn out to be false. Ron remembers just such an occurrence when he was the president of a graduate school. He had been encouraging his staff to serve the customer (the student) by being attentive and supportive. During a staff meeting someone came in and told Ron, "You are urging us to serve the students, but I was just in the bookstore and the manager wouldn't even talk to the students. They asked questions and all he did was to point them toward various resources." Ron was livid. He marched to the bookstore to chew out the manager. Right before he got to the store, his vice president for the bookstore division passed him. Ron stopped him and said, "Gus, I want you to come with me. Your bookstore manager is being so insensitive to some of our students that he isn't even talking to them."

"Ron, he has laryngitis!" Gus responded.

Man, did Ron feel small and stupid. He had assumed the worst.

The same misperceptions happen with fathers and sons. Don't ever assume that the other person meant something negatively without knowing the facts. Fathers, if your son comes home from a bad day at school and rudely says that he doesn't want to talk about it, don't assume that he's angry with you. Chances are that he's still too caught up in the frustrations of the day to talk right then.

You see, trusting one another is about having enough faith in the other person to put aside any assumptions. It will build unity in your relationship together.

Putting This to Work

1. How do you feel when someone misreads your motives or assumes the worst about something you said? For example, you say you're too tired to do something, and the other person assumes you don't like him any more. Give an illustration if that's happened to you and explain how you felt.

_____

_____

_____

✎   2. Fill in the following statements:

• I don't feel trusted by my dad/son when . . .

_____

_____

_____

• I would feel more trusted by my dad/son if he . . .

_____

_____

_____

✓   3. Commit to believe the best and trust your dad/son for one
        week. Share each evening how you both feel you are doing.

📖   4. Read 1 Corinthians 13:4–7. Discuss ways that show you
        love and trust each other.

Session 7:
Yield to Each Other

Men tend to see the word *yield* as a four-letter word. Yielding
seems to imply that we are weak, in the wrong, and afraid. But this
isn't true. Yielding is actually about strength of character and genuine, sincere love for others, whether or not they deserve it. Yielding
doesn't mean that you're a wimp. Instead, it helps provide unity in
your relationships.

Picture this, Dad: you told your son an hour ago that you'd play
basketball with him in fifteen minutes. He's been outside practicing
and shooting around, waiting for you. When you finally go out, your
son says, "Dad, you said you'd be out in fifteen minutes. I've been

waiting here for an hour!" Your immediate response is probably defensive. "You should be glad I'm out here at all. I've been stuck inside paying the bills that put clothes on your back and food on the table!" Do you know what this communicates to your son? Your son hears, "You're not important enough for me to be out playing basketball. My work and time are much more important than you, and you're out of line to be criticizing me like that." This is the message your words communicate to him.

Of course, you may have had a good excuse and your son was perhaps a little inconsiderate in his criticism of you. Instead of arguing, however, strengthen your position as a father and give your son respect by modeling humility for him. This can be done by simply apologizing. If you tell your son you will do something (in this case, play basketball) but don't do it, you need to say, "I'm sorry. It was wrong of me not to do what I said I'd do." Don't make excuses or turn the tables and accuse your son of messing up (arguing "But you had a bad attitude!"). The point is to humbly acknowledge where *you* are wrong in the situation—that's yielding. By yielding, you care for and genuinely love your son, building unity.

Let's put the shoe on the other foot, Son. Suppose your dad came out to play ball late and then yelled at you for criticizing him. You could yell back and get into a raging verbal war. But if you wanted to practice sincerely caring for your dad, you'd want to yield and not allow the argument to escalate. Show your dad some love and respect because you want to build unity into your relationship and maximize your own life. Yielding doesn't mean you never voice your disappointments; it means that you choose your words and time carefully and take into consideration what's going on in the other person's life.

We guarantee that if you yield to your dad/son in a potentially combustible situation, he would be amazed and proud. Remember that yielding is not playing dead. It's not even saying that everything is your fault. It is, however, recognizing the need your dad/son has to be encouraged and cared for at that point. Be his *friend* and yield.

Putting This to Work

 1. Have you ever heard about the game of "chicken"? In this incredibly dangerous game, two cars speed toward each other. The absurd point is to see who first swerves out of the path of the oncoming car. If you don't yield your position, you may die. Life is a lot like that: if you demand your rights, you may win the battle but lose the war. Think of the last time you had a conflict and demanded your own way. What happened? How did you feel about winning or losing? Did it really matter? Did your response help build unity or disharmony?

_____

_____

_____

_____

_____

_____

_____

✎ 2. What are two characteristics in your father/son that cause
        you to get defensive, irritated, or stubborn? List these and
        identify a recent example of each.

        1. _____

           _____

           _____

           _____

        2. _____

           _____

           _____

           _____

📖 3. Read Philippians 2:3–4. Discuss the above issues. The next
        time one of these issues comes up, how can you yield?
        Think of very specific steps you can take (bite your lip, look
        at your father's/son's perspective, ask questions, practice
        "giving up your rights", etc.). Brainstorm.

FINAL PROJECT: ZERO IN ON CARING FOR PEOPLE

The goal of this project is to focus on harmony in the home.
Remember, you and your dad/son and other members of the family
may all represent different instruments in the band. The question is,
are you all playing in the same key—harmoniously?

Every day for twenty-one days, evaluate how well you did at cre-
ating unity and harmony in your home. Don't just look at staying
out of conflicts, but evaluate how you apply each of the five UNITY

principles. Be sure to practice at least one of the principles with at least one member of your family each day.

Uplift each other.

Need each other.

Intimately relate to each other.

Trust each other.

Yield to each other.

Keep a daily log of what you did and how well it worked, and share daily with each other. Keep up the encouragement. Remember, you are working on skill development. So practice, practice, practice.

Day	Practice
1	_____
2	_____
3	_____
4	_____
5	_____
6	_____
7	_____
8	_____
9	_____
10	_____
11	_____
12	_____
13	_____
14	_____
15	_____
16	_____
17	_____
18	_____
19	_____
20	_____
21	_____

CHAPTER NINE

ENERGIZE
INTERNALLY

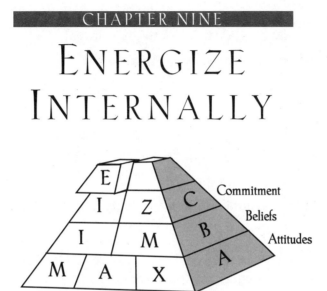

Facing an early death from brain cancer, "bad boy" Lee Atwater, President George Bush's 1988 campaign manager, found his perspective changed:

> The '80's were about acquiring—
> acquiring wealth, power, prestige. I
> know. I acquired more wealth,
> power and prestige than most. But
> you can acquire all you want and
> still feel empty. What power
> wouldn't I trade for a little more
> time with my family? What price
> wouldn't I pay for an evening with

friends? It took a deadly illness to put me eye to eye with that truth, but it is a truth that the country, caught up in its ruthless ambitions and moral decay, can learn on my dime. I don't know who will lead us through the '90's , but they must be made to speak to this spiritual vacuum at the heart of American society, this tumor of the soul.[1]

Lee Atwater was a man who knew total success from the world's standards. He was also a man who knew the futility of it all. He realized that to maximize our lives, we need to keep nourishing the roots of our spiritual lives and our character. The roots are our source of strength. We think the principle of energizing the inner life (your character and spiritual life) is the most important one you'll find in this book.

In my book *Make a Life, Not Just a Living*, I (Ron) tell this story about the core of energizing one's inner life:

> One of my favorite characters in all of history is the Jewish King Solomon. Nearly three thousand years ago he reigned as Israel's wisest and most magnificent king. Early in his career, according to the Bible, God appeared to him in a dream and asked him to make a wish. He only requested an understanding heart that he might rule with justice. People from around the world came to consult this great king. He had it all! Consider this list. He was an expert in botany and zoology, an author of three thousand proverbs, more than one thousand songs (Proverbs, Song of Solomon, Ecclesiastes), a builder of magnificent cities and structures (the temple and Solomon's palace), a man of unparalleled wealth in his time (fourteen hundred chariots, twelve thousand horsemen), and the husband of

seven hundred wives and suitor of three hundred concu-
bines.

But even though he had it all, he departed from his spiritual roots,
which led to his moral demise. The ultimate result was a divided
kingdom, a lost empire, family destruction, personal depression,
shame, and grief.

Summing up all of his life (with all the worldly treasures it gave
him), he said, "Meaningless! Meaningless! All is meaningless . . . a
chasing after the wind." At the end of the Book of Ecclesiastes, he
shares his final words of wisdom: "Now all has been heard; here is
the conclusion of the matter: Fear God and keep his commandments, for this is the whole duty of man. For God will bring every
deed into judgment including every hidden thing, whether it is good
or evil" (Eccles. 12:13–14).

Solomon's point is that, when all's said and done, there are just
two things to do in life: "fear God" (cultivate your spirituality) and
"keep his commandments" (obey truth from the heart—cultivate
character).

This chapter will develop the MAXIMIZERS principle of energizing internally.

SESSION 1:
THE SECRET TO POWER

Why is energizing the inner life so vital? Well, first of all, it is the
source of our strength. Unfortunately, recent years have shown this
strength to be lacking in many Americans.

Your roots reveal who you are at the core; if your roots are strong,
you will find strength. Of course, if your roots are weak, your life will
be just as weak. You need to ask yourself if there are any areas in your
life—or *how many* areas in your life—in which your roots are weak

or nonexistent. You can't energize the inner life if you don't know what parts need extra energy.

So what are the roots in your life? Better yet, what is your power source? Where do you go for strength and sustaining power when you need help?

We have learned how desperately we need God as our ultimate root. We simply foul up when we don't focus on him and his power. We lose perspective, we become selfish, and we slowly self-destruct.

Second, energizing the inner life is the *basis for enduring societies.* Before America even became a country, its settlers had energized inner spiritual lives. In the 1770s, the United States had a population of about three million people, yet they produced such great men as Thomas Jefferson, George Washington, John Adams, James Monroe, and James Madison. What about today? Who do we have? Can you think of a single person in the class of those men?

As Americans have refused to energize internally, they have ceased to be great and to live truly maximized lives. Our nation's founders led lives that focused on the spiritual. Abraham Lincoln once said, "The only assurance of our nation's safety is to lay our foundation in morality and religion." This is still true today. Our country will again be great when she returns to her spiritual and ethical roots. The same holds true for you.

Finally, energizing the inner life is the *secret to your satisfaction.* This internal energizing—this character-centeredness—will actually make you happy! You will be happy because you will be balanced and living with a sense of direction. You will be going somewhere instead of just staying busy. Remember the illustration of the car battery from chapter 2.

Numerous studies have shown that spiritually committed people are literally happier, more content, and more satisfied than nonspiritual people. What about you? Are you happy and content? Is your life satisfying and balanced? We know it can be if you energize internally.

Putting This to Work

1. Read 2 Corinthians 4:7. What is the true source of power?

2. Where and when do you sense you need more internal strength or power?

_____

_____

_____

_____

3. What role do character issues and the spiritual life have in holding together your family, friendships, and community?

_____

_____

_____

4. Are you fulfilled, happy, and satisfied? Where are you most satisfied? Where are you least satisfied?

_____

_____

_____

_____

SESSION 2:
THE ROLE OF FAITH

The issues of spiritual roots and character concern the core of your life. Your core could be self, money, time, an object, a person, your family, ideas, or God.

The question we want you to consider is, *What does faith offer?* Why do researchers find such positive links among faith, mental health, and happiness? It is because faith and spirituality provide a place to belong (community), a sense of purpose (commitment), and a perspective on life (contentment).

In his outstanding book *The Pursuit of Happiness,* David Myers addresses what makes people happy. He subtitles his book, "Discovering the pathway to fulfillment, well-being and enduring personal joy."

Dr. Myers takes a scientific research approach to measuring happiness in this heavily documented work. His discoveries very much align with my (Ron's) research on authentic success. He concludes that happiness and fulfillment are the by-products of certain attitudes and perspectives and are not significantly affected by externals.[2]

The Gallup Organization interviewed a cross section of Americans, comparing those low in "spiritual commitment" (people who consistently disagree with statements such as, "God loves me even though I may not always please him" and "My religious faith is the most important influence in my life") with highly spiritual people (who consistently agree with the aforementioned statements). Their finding: the highly spiritual Americans were twice as likely to say they were "very happy."[3]

Faith also provides a sense of community. People uniting under a shared belief make each other feel at home, thinking, *These people really understand me and I can talk to them.* Houses of faith (churches, synagogues, mosques, etc.) breed this sense of belonging, supporting and energizing people. There is nothing like having a *sense of belonging*, feeling people really want and need you. Maybe dads get that sense of community from their place of work. Maybe sons get it from their friends or a sports team. Such relationships make us feel secure, content, and important. And faith is the biggest community provider of them all.

The second thing faith offers is a *sense of purpose*—a commitment worth dying for. People of faith are committed to internal energizing, which produces this sense of purpose. After all, everyone at one time or another asks, "What's the meaning of life?" Faith comes when people have found some clue to this question. We can't find it in ourselves because it's found in faith in God. Rabbi Harold Kushner says, "My religious faith . . . satisfies . . . the most fundamental human need of all. That is the need to know that somehow we matter, that our lives mean something, count as something more than just a momentary blip in the universe."[4] When it comes down to it, people want their lives to count. Religious faith makes lives count.

Finally, spiritual faith gives *perspective on life*, which breeds contentment. With the sense of faith in the future that spirituality provides, we have the proper perspective of who we are in an eternal spectrum and what matters beyond the grave. People with spiritual faith seem to be the happiest and the most content because they take the focus off themselves and put it on others and the treasure of eternity.

What about you? Are you happy and content? Why or why not? As we attain a more proper perspective on life, our focus shifts. If you aren't happy and content, ask yourself where your focus is. True spiritual faith will give you a proper perspective on life and enable you to energize internally.

Putting This to Work

1. What is the center or core of your life? What is most important to you? Why?

   _____

   _____

   _____

   _____

2. Where do you get your sense of belonging or community (close friends, family, work, community, etc.)? Why do these people fill this need and how?

   _____

   _____

   _____

   _____

3. Does your faith affect your sense of purpose and direction? If so, why and how? If not, do you sense this need?

   _____

   _____

   _____

   _____

✎   4. What role does your faith play in the area of your perspec-
         tive and contentment? Do you believe in a God who
         "works all things together for good"?

         _____

         _____

         _____

         _____

☞   5. Discuss your answers with your dad/son.

📖   6. Read Hebrews 11. How is faith defined and practiced in
         that chapter?

SESSION 3:
THE FOCUS ON CHARACTER

Now that we've established the need to be constantly energizing
the inner life, how do we do it? Well, energizing the inner life con-
sists of two things. First is the need to concentrate on being. The
second thing to do is cultivate spirituality.

Concentrating on *being* basically boils down to this question: Are
you the same person in private as you are in public? This is a character question, and to energize the inner life you have to focus on
character. Your character must remain consistent.

How familiar does this sound? At school or work you are a great
guy. You are nice and helpful all day long, but the minute you get
home your attitude is awful. You complain and are impatient. Two
completely different characters show up. If you want your character
to be of the highest quality, you have to be authentic. In other
words, your character needs to be the same all the time. Coming

home to an emotionally comfortable place does not allow you to be rude.

Integrity is what you need to properly energize the inner life. Integrity in this sense means consistency—being the same in private as you are in public.

In the *Make a Life* book, Ron shares a *National Racquetball* magazine article about the story of Reuben Gonzales who was in the finals match of a professional racquetball tournament. It was Gonzales' first shot at a victory on the pro circuit, and he was playing the perennial champion. In the fifth and final game, at match point, Gonzales made a super "kill" shot into the front wall to win it all. The referee called it good. One of the two linesmen affirmed that the shot was in. But Gonzales, after a moment's hesitation, turned around, shook his opponent's hand, and declared that his shot had "skipped" into the wall, hitting the court floor first. As a result, he lost the match. He walked off the court. Everybody was stunned.

The next issue of *National Racquetball* displayed Reuben Gonzales on its front cover. The editorial searched for an explanation of this first-ever occurrence on the professional racquetball circuit. Who could ever imagine it in any sport or endeavor? A player, with everything officially in his favor, with victory in his hand, disqualified himself at match point and lost!

When asked why he admitted defeat, Reuben said, "It was the only thing I could do to maintain my integrity."

In my opinion, Reuben Gonzales may have lost that match, but he won something far more important: he maintained his self-respect, and he also gained the respect of his peers, his sport, and those in the general public fortunate enough to have watched his example as a role model.[5]

Gonzales' integrity led him to do the right thing, which won him the admiration of spectators. Note the steps involved: (1) he was honest, (2) he did the right thing, and (3) he gained the respect of others while maintaining his self-respect. This is the "Be-Do-Have" method of maximized living.

Unfortunately, many of us think not in the Be-Do-Have mind-set, but in the "Have-Do-Be" mind-set. For example, we believe that if only we can *have* enough money, we can *do* what we want to, and then we'll *be* happy.

But you know what? It doesn't work like that! You must *be* the right kind of person and then you will *do* the right things. The result will be that you will *have* everything you really want and need. This is the Be-Do-Have approach to life. It is a much more effective and satisfying approach to living. Gonzales understood that, which is why he won the day even though he lost the match.

Putting This to Work

Reflect on the area of character development. Answer the following questions and then discuss them. Remember, the goal is to understand where you are now and to move toward where you should be in the days to come. (You can only grow by identifying your weaknesses/soft spots first. Then, you have the freedom and clarity to move on.)

1. How are you different in private and public? What "faces" do you put on at business or community/church functions that are not reflective of how you are in private? Why do you suppose you do that?

_____

_____

☞   2. Share with your dad/son what you wrote. Tell how you see each other in this area.

✎   3. Do you focus more on having-doing-being or being-doing-having? How do you know? Write down at least one illustration from each of these three areas: work/school, home, and your social setting (friends).

_____

_____

_____

_____

• work/school

_____

_____

_____

• home

_____

_____

_____

• social setting (friends)

_____

_____

_____

✎ 4. What will you do this week to practice *being* (refuse to pretend to be someone else, read through this chapter daily, talk to your father/son daily)?

_____

_____

_____

☞ 5. Share with each other why you wrote what you wrote.

✎ 6. Look at the following list of character qualities. Rate yourself and your father/son on each of these. Use red pen for you and a blue pen for your father/son. Rate both of you on each quality on a scale of 1 (weak) to 10 (strong).

	Weak									Strong
Moral purity	1	2	3	4	5	6	7	8	9	10
Humility	1	2	3	4	5	6	7	8	9	10
Self-control	1	2	3	4	5	6	7	8	9	10
Perseverance	1	2	3	4	5	6	7	8	9	10
Goodness	1	2	3	4	5	6	7	8	9	10
Kindness	1	2	3	4	5	6	7	8	9	10
Integrity	1	2	3	4	5	6	7	8	9	10
Love	1	2	3	4	5	6	7	8	9	10

✓ 7. Identify one of the above characteristics (try your weakest one) to work on this next week. Mentally rehearse the right actions at least four times a day and practice them at home, school/work, and in some social setting.

📖 8. Read 2 Peter 1:5–11. What character qualities are critical?

SESSION 4: CULTIVATION OF SPIRIT

Do you consider yourself religious? Do you consider yourself spiritual? Do you know the difference?

The second key ingredient to energizing the inner life is cultivating spirituality. Notice, we did not say "being religious"—there's a big difference. Spirituality involves a personal, intimate, trusting, and loving relationship with God. Religiosity, however, involves following the rules. Spirituality is internal; religiosity is external.

Whether or not you consider yourself spiritual, you have to realize that you simply can't get through life by yourself. If you try to live on your own strength, you will fail. We've learned this over and over again. We have both given our lives to Christ. We came to the place where we understood our need for forgiveness because of our own selfishness and sin. We then invited Christ into our lives where he began a transforming work.

And yet, we have also learned how easy it is to attempt to run our own lives and miss God's best for us. I (Ron) have lived as a Christian since the age of thirteen, but there have been times of rebellion, hardness of heart, and trying it on my own. Whenever that happens (and it still does occasionally), I make poor decisions and hurt others and myself.

What astounds me the most is that God so freely forgives me and allows me to start fresh. Can you imagine starting with a clean slate, with nothing held against you? The Bible says that once we come to know Christ as our Savior, our "sins and our lawless acts [he] will remember no more" (Heb. 10:17). God not only erases the blackboard. He throws it away. It's gone. I'm forgiven. Now that isn't fair, but that's God's grace. And as you combine this sense of forgiveness along with the power of God's Holy Spirit, then you have a real power base from which to live and grow.

The only way to cultivate spirituality is to learn to experience God. One of the easiest ways to experience God is through *prayer*. When we say experience, we mean knowing God and being able to attain intimacy with him. Prayer usually involves four elements, as the A.C.T.S. acronym shows:

Adoration

Confession

Thanksgiving

Supplication

Adoration is focusing on and praising God for who he is. *Confession* involves admitting anything in your life that is wrong and that hinders your relationship with a perfect God and then accepting total, unconditional forgiveness. *Thanksgiving* is thanking God for everything you've been blessed with—health, family, friends, everything! And *supplication* is asking God to meet your needs and the needs of others.

You can also cultivate spirituality by *meditating*. Meditation involves filling yourself with and focusing on what is true and good. Meditation can be likened to a cow ruminating on her food. She chews grass, swallows it, and coughs it up again. Then she chews it, swallows it into another compartment of her stomach, and coughs it up again. (Sounds disgusting, we agree!) She keeps doing this until it goes into many parts of her system. This is exactly what we are to do with truth. We must not just hear it or read it. We must think on it over and over again. We must practice it until it becomes part and parcel of our entire lives.

Set aside some quiet time every day to fill your head with positive and uplifting thoughts and chew them over. We like to dwell on Scriptures:

> "Trust in the Lord with all your heart and lean not on your own understanding; in all your ways acknowledge him and he will make your paths straight." (Prov. 3:5–6)

> "And we know that in all things God works for the good of those who love him, who have been called according to his purpose." (Rom. 8:28)

We also like great quotes, like this one from Mother Theresa: "He who is filled with joy, preaches without words."

Finally, you build your spiritual life by *expressing faith* in your daily life. As you depend more on God, you draw closer to Him.

Faith is like a muscle. It must be exercised. You do this by continually believing in things that seem impossible. But remember that your faith is only as good as its object. You must work on getting to know God and on following a system of faith that is credible in that it answers the major issues in your life (how do I handle my soft spots and gain forgiveness? how do I handle eternity? and how do I gain purpose in my life?) and has a track record of changed lives (that you have witnessed).

Learn to concentrate on *being* and cultivate spirituality in your life, and you will begin to energize the inner life.

Putting This to Work

1. What is your view of God? What is your relationship to God like? How could you strengthen this relationship?

_____

_____

_____

_____

_____

✎ 2. What are your present practices in the three areas we have
       discussed in this session—prayer, meditation, and practic-
       ing faith?

_____

_____

_____

☞ 3. Share specifically what you both do spiritually. Discuss
       what you'd like to do in the days to come. Maybe you need
       to find a mentor to help you. Or perhaps you will want to
       do some things, such as praying, together. Don't worry
       about trying to be perfect. Your dad/son may not be as
       advanced in some of these areas as you are. Just learn
       together, building each other up.

📖 4. Read Matthew 7:16–19. How critical are your spiritual
       roots?

FINAL PROJECT: ENERGIZE INTERNALLY

The key to your power in life is to focus on the roots of your character and build your spirit. Your spirit is built as you pray, meditate,
and practice faith.

Seek to get a little closer to God every day during the next
twenty-one days by practicing praying, meditating, and developing
your faith. Keep a record of what happens and report to each other
daily.

Day   **Practice**

1   _____

2   _____

3   _____

4   _____

5   _____

6   _____

7   _____

8   _____

9   _____

10   _____

11   _____

12   _____

13   _____

14   _____

15   _____

16   _____

17   _____

18   _____

19   _____

20   _____

21   _____

CHAPTER TEN

REALIGN
RIGOROUSLY

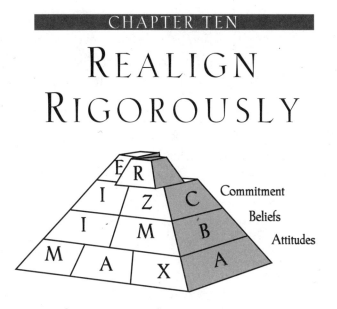

SESSION 1: INTRODUCTION

You have undoubtedly heard the statement that the shortest distance between two
points is a straight line. Although that is true,
a straight line is not always the best way to
get to where you're going. Imagine this:
you've hiked three miles to a large, deep,
beautiful lake, and you're starving. Right
across the lake you see a red-and-white
checkered blanket and a mountain of food all
set out for you. You realize you would have to
walk directly across the lake if you took the
shortest distance to the food. Since this

option would likely lead to drowning, you wisely choose to go around the lake, rather than try swimming across it.

The same principle holds true in everyday life. You're kidding yourself if you think that you'll never have to make midcourse corrections or realignments. There are obstacles everywhere—people, time, energy, money, and so on. You have to become an expert at knowing when and how to realign rigorously. Because the world changes, you have to change. How to make these midcourse corrections will be our focus in this chapter.

This task requires three critical steps—framing, focusing, and flexing—which will be discussed later in this chapter.

Putting This to Work

☞   1. Go to an arcade together. Each of you play one of the car games twice—the ones with two speeds, a steering wheel, and a gas pedal. Once you're done, go out for ice cream and answer these questions:

- Framing Questions

  1. What was your purpose in playing the game?

  2. When you were driving the car, what were your priorities? (What were you trying to do?)

  3. What were your guidelines as you went around the course? (What were you trying not to do?)

  4. What unique talents made you better or worse than your father/son?

- Focusing Question

  1. How did you see everything you needed to see while focusing on qualifying for/winning the race?

- Flexing Question

    1. In what ways did you continue to adjust as you went around the track?

✎ 2. Now write down the three key skills to making midcourse corrections on a 3" x 5" card—framing, focusing, and flexing. Daily try to use these skills (as you did on the raceway) to handle the circumstances of the day. Keep sharing what you learn.

SESSION 2: FRAMING

Suppose you found a mound of sand in your backyard. Could you make a square pile of sand that is three inches high at every point—if you are not allowed to use wood or anything as a border?

We need borders for a sandbox just as we need borders for life.

If you want to compete in sports, you have to know where the boundaries are (e.g., sidelines and end zones in football). The same is true of midcourse corrections. If you want to realign rigorously, you have to know the boundaries or framework of the given situation.

Let's consider the four areas of framing to master.

First, when making midcourse corrections, it's vital that you look at your *purpose* as it relates to the decision and to your overall mission in life. Ask yourself what you're trying to do in this decision. For example, you may be deciding if you should try out for the basketball team at your school. If part of your overall purpose is to make things happen, then maybe you should try out for the team. You realign according to what your purpose is.

Second, much of your decision-making should be based on what your *priorities* are. If you value schoolwork over basketball and realize that playing on the team could jeopardize your schoolwork, then you should take those priorities into consideration.

Third is *principles*. We think of principles as train tracks. Tracks are what the trains run on; they give trains a means to get to a destination and keep trains from wandering off in any direction. You can't get anywhere without the tracks. The same is true for our principles. We all need to develop a set of principles (such as the MAXIMIZERS principles) to guide us. Then we can realign appropriately and move along at a better pace.

Fourth, you've got to understand your own *peculiarities*—your strengths and weaknesses. We talked about these in chapter 3 when we focused on achieving personal significance. Fathers and sons need to help each other recognize particular strengths, weaknesses, consistencies, and inconsistencies. Then each can help the other make midcourse corrections. If you know your peculiarities, you can decide on issues easier.

Putting This to Work

1. Read Proverbs 4:20–27. What were Solomon's "framing" guidelines for life?

2. Your assignment is to apply the four principles of purpose, priorities, principles, and peculiarities to some area where you need to make a change. Let's say that you haven't been focusing enough on building a team within your family. How do you make an adjustment based on this framework? Let us illustrate.

   You begin with purpose. What is your purpose? How does that affect the family? Write down your thoughts.

   _____

   _____

_____

_____

_____

What are your priorities and how do they influence the family? This will force you to really evaluate what is important. If you don't, you'll continue to focus on things that aren't as high a priority as your own family.

Where do your principles fit in? What are they? Is commitment to the family one of your core principles? How do the MAXIMIZERS principles affect building a team? Brainstorm this area for a moment.

_____

_____

_____

_____

Finally, how do your peculiar strengths and weaknesses influence team building? Perhaps you are strong at encouraging and weak at listening. What do you need to do with your peculiarities to strengthen the teamness in your family?

_____

_____

_____

_____

Get together for a few minutes every day this week to check up on each other.

SESSION 3: FOCUSING

According to Robert Ringer in his book *Million Dollar Habits*, "Laserlike focus is perhaps the most common trademark of the supersuccessful." He clearly details the progression of what will happen when you narrow and commit to your focus:

> The more certain you are about your purpose in life, the more focused you'll be on living in the present and the more enthusiastic you'll be in your day-to-day work . . . the more likely you will attract the attention of positive, enthusiastic people; the more positive, enthusiastic people you attract, the more successful you'll be; and the more successful you are, the more present-living oriented and enthusastic you'll be. Thus you set in motion a self-perpetuating cycle of enthusiasm and success.[1]

Wouldn't you like this to be true in your life?

The second vital part of realigning rigorously is learning to focus. Focusing is keeping in mind what you want to do and what your overall purpose is, while being aware of the circumstances and specifics of your surroundings. In order to focus, you have to learn how to *concentrate*. You have to pay attention and carefully observe your environment. When you concentrate, you limit your thinking to one or two issues.

I (Ron) heard a story some years ago about concentration that grabbed my attention. A chemist wanted to teach his students the power of observation and focus, so during one class, he told his students, "Do exactly as I do." Then he took a specimen bottle filled with—you guessed it—specimen, stuck his forefinger in the bottle, took it out, and put his middle finger in his mouth. Then he repeated his command of doing exactly as he had done to his amazed students. The students freaked out! They thought he had stuck his forefinger in the specimen bottle, then put that same finger in his mouth. The bottle was passed around, and one by one, the students did just as they thought their professor had done. It was disgusting. Then the professor said, "Ladies and gentlemen, you've got to focus. You got so disgusted by what you *thought* I was doing that you didn't notice that I stuck one finger in the specimen bottle and a different finger in my mouth." Learn to concentrate.

If you want to focus, you also have to be *constantly learning*. Getting out of high school or college doesn't mean that your learning is over for life. You should be seeking every day to learn something new and to apply it to your life.

The goal of constantly learning can be a deceptive one, however. We're introduced to an enormous amount of new information every day, but this does not constitute learning. Information can contain truth and error, and some of it can be trivial or incompatible to what we want to achieve in life. Learning, however, involves understanding the information and building what's good and true into our lives in an appropriate way.

How can we make sure that we are constantly learning? First of all, we have to comprehend what is important for us to know. For instance, you should know things that relate to your mission statement (see chapter 6, "March to a Mission").

Next, you need to understand what all the information you're reading or studying about really means. It's not enough to simply know facts; you need to look into the information and see how it affects you, why it matters, and so forth. Finally, once you've examined the information, you need to decide what to do with it. How does this information apply to your life? Decide how you can implement it into your life. Then you'll begin to focus your life and effectively realign rigorously.

Putting This to Work

1. Read Hebrews 12:1–3. How did Jesus focus? What difference did it make?

2. To test your ability to focus, spend three minutes outside with your eyes shut and afterward make a note of every sound you heard. Then, spend three minutes outside looking around you, identifying every shade of color you can, and later write these down. Discuss what you observed. How well did you focus?

_____

_____

_____

_____

_____

3. List a brand new insight you have learned in each of these areas in the past month:

   • Yourself

_____

_____

   • Your father/son

_____

_____

• Your family

_____

_____

• A friend

_____

_____

• Your future

_____

_____

Now discuss your answers.

☞ 4. Brainstorm at least five ways you can both continue to learn and grow over this next year.

1. _____

_____

2. _____

_____

3. _____

_____

4. _____

_____

5. _____

_____

Now put the above ideas into practice. Encourage each other and ask about your father's/son's progress.

SESSION 4: FLEXING

Change is inevitable. The modern world is phenomenally complex and chaotic, constantly forcing us to make midcourse corrections. Change is the only way we'll keep from becoming out-of-date. Three tools are needed to remain flexible: creativity, adaptability, and the ability to learn from mistakes.

We live in a world that is not conducive to *creativity*. People are uncomfortable with new ideas and anything that does not correspond with the status quo.

At the turn of the twentieth century, Charles H. Duell, head of the U.S. Patent Office, recommended to President McKinley that the Patent Office be closed down because "everything that can be invented, has already been invented." How wrong he was! He had gotten stuck in status quo thinking and had not given enough credit to human creativity.

Creativity is the ability to see things in a new way, taking a fresh look at the familiar. Public relations executive John Budd writes, "Creativity is the result of intense focus on a particular problem. It's a logical thought process that maneuvers towards a solution. It occurs not because a person is trying to be original but because a person is attempting something difficult. A truly creative person excludes conventional solutions and searches beyond them."[2]

In addition to creativity, you need *adaptability* to be flexible. Adaptability means being able to adjust to people or circumstances around us. At UCLA, Matt had two roommates. As he got to know the guys, he saw that he and his roommates needed to adapt certain behaviors and attitudes to ensure that their living together would be a positive experience. Both he and his roommates made some mistakes on the way, but they learned to correct the situation, thereby discovering the practical value of adaptability.

Finally, although few people see the need to *learn from their mistakes*, mistakes provide valuable lessons, and we need to be flexible enough to learn from them. A mistake is a wasted opportunity if you don't learn from it.

Buckminster Fuller is best known for inventing the geodesic dome, the honeycomb sphere that encases many radar stations and contained the U.S. Pavilion at the 1967 World's Fair in Montreal. He's also known for targeting his ingenuity to almost every practical aspect of living. But his inventions were less important to him than his lifelong refinement of the insights that made them a reality. Fuller spent the last fifty years of his life delivering one critical message: "Humans have learned only through mistakes. . . . The billions of humans in history have had to make quadrillions of mistakes to have arrived at the state where we now have 150,000 common words to identify the many unique and only metaphysically comprehensible nuances of experience. . . . The courage to adhere to the truth, as we learn it, involves then the courage to face ourselves with the clear admission of all the mistakes we have made. Mistakes are sins only when not admitted."[3]

Making mistakes while playing tennis has taught me (Ron) how to constantly flex and adjust. To be effective in tennis you must admit your mistakes and take responsibility for them. I was fascinated during the five sets I played recently to hear the various excuses made for bad shots. Here are a few of them. As you read them, think about who or what was blamed for the mistakes.

That ____ racket!

That ____ sun!

I stayed up too late!

These new shoes just don't work!

Why don't you watch the ball! (to the partner)

Those guys are so _____ lucky! (referring to the opponents)

Shut up out there! (to the loud spectators)

I'm just too tired.

This coffee hasn't kicked in yet.

I guess I'm getting old.

These pants are too tight.

Let's get some new tennis balls.

My mind just doesn't function.

My muscles cramped.

My foot's sore.

My back hurts.

Those guys have to be blind!

Something's wrong with that net!

You sure that line's straight back there?

Boy, this sun is right in my eyes.

The sweat's dripping into my eyes and I can't see.

My glasses are fogged up.

How about you? Do you take responsibility for your life? Do you admit your own faults and weaknesses, then respond in a creative and adaptable way? Are you flexible in your life?

Putting This to Work

1. How creative are you? For instance, are you good at coming up with new ways to solve problems? What was the last creative thing you did?

_____

_____

_____

☞   2. Brainstorm seven creative ways you can spend time as a
        family this week, even if it's just fifteen minutes. None of
        the activities can be the same, and each experience must be
        fun. At least three of these times must be away from the
        home. Also try to limit your creative activities to one per
        day. Record your ideas.

Day   **Fun Activity**

1   _____

2   _____

3   _____

4   _____

5   _____

6   _____

7   _____

✓   3. Now put your creative ideas into action. Also, keep discuss-
        ing how your ideas are working out and whether you need
        to make some midcourse corrections.

FINAL PROJECT: REALIGN RIGOROUSLY

Think of a decision the family needs to make (moving, vacation-
ing, buying a house). For the next twenty-one days, apply the three
basic skills of framing, focusing, and flexing to this decision.

Framing

- Purpose: How does the purpose and mission of the family and the various individuals in it affect this decision?

- Priorities: What are your family priorities? What difference do these make to your decision?

- Principles: How do the various MAXIMIZERS principles affect the decision?

- Peculiarities: How do the unique traits of the family members affect this decision?

Focusing

What are the important issues to keep in mind as you look at this decision (e.g., feelings of family members, financial concerns, family unity, etc.)?

Flexing

Brainstorm ways to look at the decision and creative alternatives to the decision.

Now write down the decision to be made. Log your application of the three midcourse correction skills.

Decision: _____

_____

_____

_____

_____

_____

_____

Day	How I applied framing, focusing, and flexing
1	_____
2	_____
3	_____
4	_____
5	_____
6	_____
7	_____
8	_____
9	_____
10	_____
11	_____
12	_____
13	_____
14	_____
15	_____
16	_____
17	_____
18	_____
19	_____
20	_____
21	_____

CHAPTER ELEVEN

STAYING THE COURSE

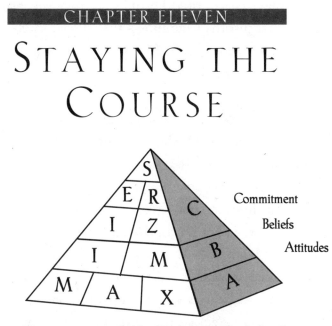

Commitment

Beliefs

Attitudes

Have you ever had a bad day? "Bad day?" you say. "What about a bad week, bad month, or bad year?"

We all have those bad times that cause us to feel discouraged, overwhelmed, frustrated, and hopeless.

A great example of this kind of day can be found in the story of *Alexander and the Terrible, Horrible, No Good, Very Bad Day!* by Judith Viorst.

> I went to sleep with gum in my mouth and now there's gum in my

hair and when I got out of bed this morning I tripped on the skateboard and by mistake I dropped my sweater in the sink while the water was running and I could tell it was going to be a terrible, horrible, no good, very bad day.[1]

And that was just the beginning—the character's day went from bad to worse. Have you ever had a day like that? Sure you have. The principle of staying the course is all about how we deal with those tough days.

It's easy to do a good job at maximizing your life when things are going well. But what about when the circumstances of your life are not so great? If you're like us, your reaction during these down times might involve getting angry, rolling up into a little ball and going to sleep, or sitting in front of the TV.

Although there are plenty of bad days, we cannot really control the things that happen to us. What we *can* do, however, is stay the course. We can persevere. *When it comes down to it, we think that perseverance during difficulties is what separates ordinary people from extraordinary people.* Notice the beginning of the word *extraordinary*—*extra*. People who want to maximize their lives keep giving that extra in all they do. They stay the course. They don't quit. They make things happen and march to a mission.

This chapter will focus on three areas of persevering:
1. Fighting the good fight
2. Remaining faithful
3. Finishing the course

SESSION 1:
FIGHTING THE GOOD FIGHT

Have you ever been in a fight? Talk about it for a moment right now. What was it like? What happened? What did you do? How did you feel?

I (Ron) remember getting the stuffing knocked out of me more than once while growing up. I was a little fat guy. Kids used to pick on me, and I would get angry and go after them. But I usually got squashed in the process.

Life is a battle and the first skill to develop in persevering is to fight the good fight. We have come to think that success means being comfortable and living a calm life. However, we also think that people who have this kind of life are stuck in a rut—not growing anymore. True, it's much easier to react to everything than to make things happen. But we are engaged in a war for our hearts and minds. Look around you. Everywhere our culture attacks our hearts and minds and tries to sabotage our desire to be complete, integrity-filled men.

Sons, if you haven't yet, you will soon feel the pressures of drugs and alcohol and the push to be just like everyone else. Fathers, you know that in every arena of life there are pressures to sacrifice your integrity and sense of mission (pressure to abandon business ethics, pressure to take your focus off your family and put all your focus on your job, reading or watching the wrong things). We can't let up for one minute. We're already losing the war in many ways, so we're on the defensive. How do we get on the offensive? Oddly enough, we have to practice good defensive warfare to be able to shift to the offensive.

You can start by getting angry. No, that's not a typo. It's important to get angry at the right things, the things that are attacking your minds and hearts. It's also important to put on the appropriate armor in a defensive struggle. The armor is made of the principles for maximized living that we've talked about throughout the book, and putting it on requires a constant focus on these principles. Concentrate on the roots (which you are responsible for), not the fruit (which you aren't responsible for).

If we want to win the fight we're waging against the unprincipled, it's necessary to do three things. First, *develop a specific strategy*. You have to figure out a plan or formula for winning just like a football team. The coach has to take every position and sharpen it, and we need to do the same. By doing this, you're deepening your roots and beginning to take the offensive. Second, you need to *identify your resources*. These resources are going to help you take the offensive, providing you with the tools you need to win. Finally, you need to *cooperate as a unit*. No one can win if he fights alone. Cooperating as a unit will be tough because people like working by themselves. But we have realized that we are simply too weak to survive without the help of others. Develop an accountability group to encourage you and help you keep going. Then you are on the road to winning the fight.

Putting This to Work

1. Recall the opening story, *Alexander and the Terrible, Horrible, No Good, Very Bad Day!* by Judith Viorst, then answer the following questions: What's the worst day you can remember in your life? What happened? How did you feel?

2. What are the various enemies/forces attacking your home? Brainstorm these (television, conflict, schedules, etc.).

3. How do you use the three skills of offensive warfare (framing, focusing, and flexing) in protecting your home?

- Develop a specific strategy to win: What is yours for the family?

  _____

  _____

  _____

- Identify your resources to win: What books, tapes, friendships, spiritual resources, and so forth, can you list?

  _____

  _____

  _____

- Cooperate as a unit: Does each family member understand and practice this principle?

  _____

  _____

  _____

✓   4.   Live each day this week with this warfare mind-set, applying the above principles of offensive and defensive warfare.

📖   5.   Read 2 Corinthians 10:3–6. What is the method of warfare promoted here?

SESSION 2: REMAINING FAITHFUL

It is impossible to stay the course if you don't remain faithful. Some people tend to think that faithfulness isn't very important for maximizing one's life. They couldn't be more wrong. If staying the course is the most consistent principle in people who maximize their lives, then remaining faithful is the most important facet of staying the course. If we want to persevere, we have to stay the course. And if we want to stay the course, we have to remain faithful. Perseverance involves building right habits and principles into our lives and continuing to implement them and make them our own.

Faithfulness is one of the least revered and most needed qualities in our world culture today. To be faithful is to "adhere strictly to the person, cause, or idea to which one is bound; be dutiful and loyal." Synonyms of this word include "loyal, true, constant, steadfast, staunch, resolute," and "trustworthy."

Let's take an example of building faithfulness into your life through the development of new and lasting habits. Suppose you've identified an inappropriate response to anger as one of your soft spots and want to X out that negative. To do this, you'll have to make a conscious effort (every time you feel anger coming) to direct it with right thoughts and responses. This is something Matt struggles with in sports. When he's playing tennis and hits the ball into the net, his first response is to throw his hat down on the ground and stomp on it. He has to make a conscious effort every time he's feeling frustrated to put the situation in perspective and respond appropriately. Matt's getting better at this, but he knows that just one stomping of the hat will start him slipping back into the old habit.

We tend to think that little things don't matter in the long run. But remaining faithful in little things is exactly what distinguishes someone who is growing from someone who can never kick a bad habit, behavior, attitude, or lifestyle.

We want to suggest some specific ways to maintain faithfulness, especially to the MAXIMIZERS principles. First, *keep organizing your thinking around these principles*. We spoke earlier of writing down the MAXIMIZERS principles in the margin of the article or book you're reading. This will help you think about the principles.

Second, *develop a file system,* having one file folder for each of the ten principles, and sub-files for each of the sessions and skills we've developed in this book. This will allow you to organize various articles and other tools. As you read books and articles, mark which principle or issue is developed, copy the passage or article, and file it.

Third, write down the MAXIMIZERS acrostic on a 3" x 5" card, memorize it, and use it, to *create a grid to evaluate* discussions, advertisements, TV programs, and other sources of information. Keep asking yourself, *What principle is illustrated, violated, or ignored?*

Remember, we want you to *craft* a life, which requires faithfully practicing these principles and skills day in and day out.

Putting This to Work

1. Read Matthew 25:14–30. What is the importance of faithfulness here?

2. Choose a one-page article out of any magazine. Read it together and mark which MAXIMIZERS principles are illustrated or violated. Discuss this.

3. Identify an area in your life where you have succeeded. Discuss the obstacles you had to overcome to experience that success. Be as specific as possible.

SESSION 3: FINISHING THE COURSE

It's impossible to win a race without finishing the course. While that seems obvious, many people who supposedly want to win the race of life refuse to finish the journey.

Naturally, we all get tired, unmotivated, frustrated, and fed up. Sometimes you just want to quit what you're doing. Matt felt like that recently. After returning from a semester of demanding work, he was tired and just wanted to watch TV. He realized, however, that if he wanted to make a difference and live a whole and complete life, he needed to persevere and finish the course he had set for himself in college. At times like these we all need to be more focused and finish the task at hand.

The great inventor Thomas Edison did not give up when his first efforts to find an effective filament for the carbon incandescent lamp failed. He did countless experiments with countless kinds of materials. As each failed, he would toss it out the window. The pile reached to the second story of his house. Then he sent men to China, Japan, South America, Asia, Jamaica, Ceylon, and Burma in search of fibers and grasses to be tested in his laboratory.

One weary day on October 21, 1879—after thirteen months of repeated failures—he succeeded in his search for a filament that would stand the stress of electric current. This was how it happened: casually picking up a bit of lampblack, he mixed it with tar and rolled it into a thin thread. Then the thought occurred: why not try a carbonized cotton fiber?

For five hours he worked, but the fiber broke before he could remove the mold. At last a perfect strand emerged—only to be ruined while trying to place it inside a glass tube. Edison refused to admit defeat. He continued without sleep for two days and nights. Finally, he managed to slip one of the carbonized threads into a vacuum-sealed bulb. He turned on the current and the sight he had so long desired to see finally met his eyes. His persistence amidst such discouraging odds gave the world the wonderful electric light.[2]

Many people give up because they're discouraged. If you dissect the word *discourage*, you'll see it means without courage. People give up because they don't have the courage to finish what they've started. When you lose courage, you begin to tell yourself that you can't do it. Then you become convinced that you can't, and end up altogether hopeless.

We quit because we don't want to risk failure. Yet history has shown that success often comes after a failure—indeed, often after many failures. Don't forget the numerous defeats Abraham Lincoln experienced before becoming president.

Remember, we do those things that make sense to us and those which are pleasurable. You need to attach enough pleasure to accomplishing your goal so that you never, ever quit.

Accept the fact that sometimes you *will* fail. But you only become a *failure* when you give up. So don't give up.

Putting This to Work

1. Think of a New Year's resolution you've made about something you wanted to change in your life. How long did you stick with it? Why did you stop?

2. Identify one area in your life where you want to succeed. Write down—in detail—how you will feel and what will happen if you do succeed. Then write down—in detail—how you will feel and what will happen if you don't succeed.

📖 3. Read 2 Timothy 4:7–8. How did Paul (the author of 2 Timothy) finish his course? How will you?

FINAL PROJECT: STAYING THE COURSE

✎ 1. Write down on a 3" x 5" card the ten MAXIMIZERS principles. (Yes, we know you did this earlier—we're re-emphasizing it.) Every time you read an article/book or listen to a conversation, make a written or mental note of which principle is affected.

☞ 2. Come up with one issue you faced this week and how you applied one of the ten principles to it.

☞ 3. Brainstorm ways you can keep growing in your understanding of these principles (read a book together, listen to tapes, work on projects, etc.).

Now, DO IT! And never, ever give up! You are a team and have the opportunity to spend the rest of your lives building up one another. Just don't quit!

NOTES

Chapter 3

1. Source unknown.

Chapter 4

1. Scott Peck, *The Road Less Traveled* (New York: Simon & Schuster, 1997).

Chapter 5

1. Ken Blanchard with Norman Peale, *The Power of Ethical Management* (New York: William Morrow and Company, 1988), 30–31.

Chapter 6

1. Richard Leider, *The Power of Purpose* (New York: Fawcett Gold Medal, 1985), 3.

2. George MacDonald, *Ordering Your Private World* (Nashville, TN: Oliver-Nelson, 1984), 15.

Chapter 8

1. Paul Lewis, *Dad's Only Newsletter* (Julian, Calif.: Corporate Family Resources, 1989), 1.

Chapter 9

1. Lee Atwater with Todd Brewster, "Lee Atwater's Last Campaign," *Life*, February 1991, 67.

2. David G. Myers, *The Pursuit of Happiness* (New York: Avon Books, 1992), 179. This text analyzes the traits that lead to happiness and fulfillment by making extensive, objective usage of scientific studies conducted worldwide.

3. Cited in Myers, 3.

4. Harold Kushner, "You've God to Believe in Something," *Redbook*, December 1987, 92–94.

5. Denis Waitley, *Being the Best* (Nashville: Thomas Nelson Publishers, 1987), 58.

Chapter 10

1. Robert J. Ringer, *Million Dollar Habits* (New York: Wynwood Press, 1990), 88, 94.

2. Study guide (Arrowhead Springs, Calif.: Campus Crusade for Christ), 3.

3. Buckminster Fuller, "Mistake Mystique," *East/West*, April 1977, 26–28.

Chapter 11

1. Judith Viorst, *Alexander and the Terrible, Horrible, No Good, Very Bad Day!* (Hartford, Conn.: Atheneum Press, 1977).

2. Paul Lee Tan, *Signs of the Times* (Rockville, Md.: Assurance Publishers, 1979), 998.

If you'd like to share your thoughts about this book with us, write to us at:

Future Achievement International
12989 Abra Drive
San Diego, CA 92128

619-487-3177/fax 619-487-9212
futureone@earthlink.net

Also available from
Ron Jenson

MAKE A LIFE, NOT JUST A LIVING

10 Timeless Life Skills That Will Maximize Your Real Net Worth

Success comes not from making money, but from making a difference.

The world tends to define success in terms of power, prosperity, and pleasure. But does the pursuit of these things produce a happy life? This extraordinary book will help readers articulate and pursue a definition of success that leads to a balanced, fulfilled, and significant life. After many years of research with leaders around the world, Dr. Jenson has discovered the absolute, non-negotiable axioms that produce truly successful lives. He has rendered these into ten universal organizing principles of living which will help anyone develop wisdom and "the craftsmanship of living." Complete with true-life success stories, this inspiring book will enable you to make a good life for yourself, and that goes far beyond just making a living.

Special features include:
- •Action Steps compel readers to reflect and improve upon themselves
- •Charts and illustrations clarify the many different qualities of success
- •Features quotes from great political, literary, and financial leaders throughout history

Available at fine bookstores everywhere